CONCEPTS OF BUDDHISM

CONCEPTS OF BUDDHISM

BY

BIMALA CHURN LAW, PH. D., M. A., B. L.

Autho, of ..A History of Pali Literature", ..Life & Work of Buddhaghosa",
..Some Kastriya Tribe of Ancient India", etc/

WITH A FOREWORD BY

THE MOST HON'BLE THE MARQUESS OF ZETLAND,

SECRETARY OF STATE FOR INDIA

GYAN

ISBN : 978-81-212-0022-6

First Publication in 1882

Published by

Gyan Publishing House
5, Ansari Road
Daryaganj, New Delhi-110002
Phone: 9811692060
E-mail: books@gyanbooks.com

Printed at: G. Print Process, Delhi.

CONTENTS

FOREWORD

The stimulus given to research by the late Sir Asutosh Mukherji when as Vice-Chancellor of the Calcutta University he set on foot an ambitious scheme of postgraduate studies, has brought into existence a body of Indian research-workers who for some years past have been carrying on work first undertaken by European scholars of world-wide reputation. Prominent amongst those who have turned their attention to the early history and philosophy of the Hindus, is Dr. Bimala Churn Law who has to his credit a number of volumes throwing light on the history and culture of the peoples who, some four or five hundred years before the Christian era, inhabited that part of India of which Patna, the capital of the modern province of Bihar, is now the centre. It was here that Buddha lived and preached the doctrine of which Dr. Law gives us in the present volume a scholarly analysis based upon a careful study of the original texts.

In its main outlines the doctrine of Buddhism is now pretty widely known. But a full understanding of it must necessarily depend upon the interpretation placed upon the many technical terms and phrases in which it abounds, and it is this task of interpretation that Dr. Law sets out to discharge. It is not without significance that two of the shortest and most widely known words in the literature of Buddhism — *Dhamma* and *Nibbāna* — are precisely the words which have given rise to the greatest degree of controversy.

It is not surprising, therefore, to find that it is to the concepts indicated by these two words that Dr. Law devotes the greatest amount of space. It may be that the reader of his chapter on *Nibbāna* will leave it with the conclusion that it was not the least element in Buddha's greatness that unlike the generality of mankind — even of Buddhist mankind — he remained unmoved by the logical conclusion of the human mind, handicapped by the necessity under which it labours of functioning within the limits of time and space, that Nibbāna is the equivalent of extinction.

To follow the author in his examination of these two concepts would demand far more space than the writer of a foreword is entitled to; let me, therefore, by way of illustration of Dr. Law's analyses, take one of the less difficult of the concepts of Buddhism, namely, that of the Four Noble Truths in which are proclaimed the existence, the cause and the possibility of escape from suffering and finally the means of excape by way of the Noble Eightfold Path. The steps in the Noble Eightfold Path — right view, right resolve, right speech, etc. — are well known; what is less well known is their precise significance, and it is this that Dr. Law proceeds to explain. His analysis of the concept constituting the first of the Four Noble Truths — ***Dukkha***, the affirmation that all existence is suffering — may be taken as an example of his method. ***Dukkha*** whether of the body or of the mind is conditioned by certain circumstances, and in the absence of such circumstances it cannot occur. These circumstances may be described compendiously as the day to day experiences of conscious life; and if the succession of such experiences or happenings cannot be changed it is at least open to the harassed mortal to enquire if there be any state of consciousness, on attaining to which an individual is no longer affected by life's vicissitudes. The answer given by Buddhism affirms that there is attainable a state in which the consciousness of the individual is wholly unrelated to anything to which in life as we know it, we can apply the term „object". The tried method of reaching that state is *Jhāna* or *Samādhi*. *Jhāna* or *Samādhi* is, therefore, according to Dr. Law, the central point in the Noble Eightfold Path, the other seven practices constituting steps leading up to it. But neither *Jhāna* nor *Samādhi* is the simple concept which the above account might lead one to suppose; and Dr. Law devotes a chapter based on a wide selection of texts from the Buddhist scriptures and commentaries to a careful analysis of these essentially important terms. Here we pass into the higher realm of abstract thought, and the reader must follow carefully in the footsteps of the author himself.

I am tempted to make one further reference to the subject matter of Dr. Law's volume, namely, to his chapter on *Puggala*, in which the case for and against the existence of an individual as a permanent entity is discussed. It will be remembered how in the *Milindapañha*, or "Questions of King Milinda", the King is driven by the inexorable logic of the Sage Nāgasena into admitting that there can be no such thing as an individual soul. How then, it will naturally be asked, can there be rebirth, the chief of the evils which it is the object of the Buddhist to escape, since to speak of re-incarnation when there is no soul to take on flesh, or of transmigration when there is no entity to migrate, is merely to indulge in a contradiction in terms? Nāgasena, the Sage, had his answer; Dr. Law has his. Indeed, with happy condensation, he crystallises the Buddhist view on this vexed question in a single sentence — "With the Buddhist, rebirth is to be conceived as *Kammasantati*, or, the continuity of an impulse".

The many other concepts of Buddhism, including that of the Wheel of Causation with the twelve *nidānas* as its motive force, and the doctrine of *Kamma*, the Pali spelling and the Buddhist version of the Sanskrit doctrine of *Karma* which constitutes the warp upon which the threads of the whole variegated philosophy of Hinduism is woven, will be found similarly analysed in the pages which follow. But I have said enough, perhaps, to make it clear that scholar and layman alike will find good value in the lucid exposition of these and other concepts of Buddhism which Dr. Law gives us.

ZETLAND
16.8.1936

PREFACE

In this little treatise an attempt has been made to deal with some of the important concepts of Buddhism: Saraṇa (Profession of Faith), Pāramitā (Perfection), Jāti (Caste), Ariyasacca (Four Noble Truths), Ariya aṭṭhaṅgika Magga (Noble Eightfold Path), Jhāna (Meditation), Puggala (Individuality and Personality), Paṭiccasamuppāda (Dependent Origination), Kamma (Volition), Dhamma and Nibbāna. I must confess that it has not been an easy task to handle the subject, as the main concepts of Buddhism still require a very careful consideration before saying anything definitely about them. I have, however, spared no pains to throw some new light on the subject from the texts that have not been accorded the treatment they deserve.

I must acknowledge my gratitude to the Most Honourable The Marquess of Zetland, P.C., G.C.S.I., G.C.I.E., Secretary of State for India, who has very kindly contributed a foreword to this treatise in spite of the heavy burden of his duties. I remain ever grateful to him for the interest he takes in my researches.

The Kern Institute of Holland has done me a great honour by accepting this treatise as their monograph for which I am greatly thankful to the authorities of the Institute and especially to my esteemed friend, Professor J. Ph. Vogel, C.I.E., Ph. D.

BIMALA CHURN LAW

43, Kailas Bose Street,
Calcutta, the 9th September
1936.

CHAPTER I

SARAṆA

(*Profession of Faith*)

In popular usage the word *saraṇa* means a 'shelter', a place where a man driven by fear, seeks shelter or protection. The Buddhist texts mention mountains and forests, gardens and trees as places of shelter, which are not considered by the Buddhists to be the real places of shelter [1]. With the Buddhists the term *Saraṇas* or Refuges are the Triad: the Buddha, the Doctrine and the Order. Each of these Refuges is a supreme object of devotion and worship. The Buddha is said to have established the converts in three Saraṇas. The usual formula by which a Buddhist takes refuge in the Triad is as follows:

Buddhaṃ saraṇaṃ gacchāmi,
Dhammaṃ saraṇaṃ gacchāmi,
Saṅghaṃ saraṇaṃ gacchāmi.

This formula is recited on all solemn occasions and is thrice repeated [2].

According to Buddhaghosa and other Pāli commentators, *Saraṇāgamana* is not a mere formal recital of one's faith in the Triad but an expression of self devotion to an object and communion [3]. *Saraṇāgamana* serves to establish a relation between the worshipper and the worshipped. If a person taking refuge in the Triad is ordained as a member of the Holy Order, he is called a Bhikkhu, and if such a person sticks to household life, he is called an *Upāsaka* or layman. *Upāsanā* or an act of worship constitutes the mark of an

---

[1] *Dhammapada*, 188:
Bahuṃ ve saraṇaṃ yanti pabbatāni vanāni ca ārāmarukkhacetyāni manussā bhayatajjitā.

[2] *Vinaya, Mahāvagga*, p. 22.

[3] *Sumaṅgala-vilāsinī*, I. p. 231: *Paramatthajotikā*, I. *p. 16*: *Tappasāda-taggarukatāhi vihata-kileso tapparāyanatākārappavatto cittuppādo saraṇāgamanaṃ.*

Upāsaka [1]. *Saraṇāgamana* is of two kinds, *lokika* (common) and *lokuttara* (uncommon). *Lokika saraṇa* contemplates the tangible attributes of the Triad, while the *lokuttara saraṇa* aims at *nirvāṇa* as the supreme object of attainment [2]. Buddhaghosa speaks of the following four modes of *saraṇāgamana*:

(1) Self-dedication (*atta-sanniyyātanena*)

(2) Having the mind bent upon the object (*tapparāyanatāya*)

(3) Entering into relation as a disciple (*sissabhāvūpagamanena*)

(4) Adoration (*paṇipātena*).

The first mode is defined as conscious dedication of oneself to the Triad. The second mode consists in entertaining the Triad as the final end or ideal. The third mode consists in conscious acceptance of the position of a disciple or follower in relation to the Triad. The fourth mode consists in the act of saluting, honouring and glorifying the Triad. In following the fourth mode the devotee must believe that the object of worship is the highest of its kind (*aggadakkhiṇeyya*) [3].

Buddha, the first member of the Triad, means the Enlightened or Awakened One. According to the Upaniṣads, *Buddha* in the sense of the Awakened, occurs as a predicate of 'Soul'. *Suprabuddha* is the epithet of the *arhats* [4]. *Sammāsambuddha* and *Pacceka-Buddha* are self made personalities. They are called self-made because they attain *mukti* by their own efforts, without the aid of any teacher. A *Srāvaka Buddha* is one who has become a saint by following the teachings of a Master. A *Buddha* is also called a *Bhagavā*. According to the *Mahāniddesa* [5] and the *Paramatthajotikā* [6], the epithet, *Bhagavā*, was bestowed on the Buddha neither by his parents nor by his other relations. It was acquired by him on his attainment of omniscience. *Bhagavā* is equal to *bhagayutta*, one endowed with *bhaga*, which, in its generally accepted sense, means the sixfold supreme possession of *issariya*, *dhamma*, *yasa*, *sirī*, *kāma* and *payatana*. *Issariya* com-

---

[1] *Sumaṅgala-vilāsinī*, I. p. 234: *Upāsatīti upāsako.*

[2] *Ibidem*, I. p. 231.

[3] *Ibidem*, I. pp. 231 foll.

[4] *Dhammapada, verses* 296—301.

[5] pp. 142—143.

[6] I. pp. 107—109.

prehends the idea of such qualities as *aṇimā* and the rest. *Dhamma* means the transcendental virtues. *Yasa* implies a pure fame of universal recognition. *Siri* connotes an all-round accomplishment. *Kāma* signifies all objects of desire. *Payatana* means the supreme effort to gain sovereignty over all. Bhagavābhajī or bhattavā, one who has recourse to, i.e., has the experience of all things. *Bhagavā* = *bhāgī* means the participator of all acquisitions. *Bhagavā* = *vibhattavā* means one who explains things by apportionment or method of analytical distinction. *Bhagavā* = *bhaggakārī*, i.e., the destroyer of all evils. *Bhagavā* = *garu*, the master who is superior to all. *Bhagavā* = *bhāgyavā*, the fortunate or blessed one. *Bhagavā* = *bhavantaga*, i.e., one who has gone beyond individual existence. *Bhagavā* = *subhāvitatta*, i.e., one who has fully developed himself [1].

The following attributes are ascribed to Buddha in the tract called *Dhammādāsa* or 'Mirror of Faith': That he is the Blessed One, endowed with faculties and noble conduct, well-gone, perfect in his knowledge of the world, unsurpassed guide to persons coming in for training, a teacher to gods and men, the Enlightened One, the Master [2].

A Buddha is also called a Tathāgata for the following reasons: (1) he has come in the same way; (2) he has gone in the same way; (3) he is endowed with the sign of *tatha*; (4) he is supremely enlightened in *tathādhamma*; (5) he has seen *tathā*; (6) he preaches *tathā*; (7) he does *tathā* truthfully; and (8) he overcomes all [3].

Dhamma, the second of the Triad, signifies "a doctrine which is well-expounded, which bears fruit in this very life, which is not conditioned by time, which has 'come and see' for its motto, which leads to the destination or desired end and which is to be experienced by the wise individually" [4]. The Dhamma embodying all the tenets of the Master was to take the place of the Master in his absence. After the demise of the Buddha, one of his disciples declared: *Mayaṃ dhammapaṭisaraṇā*, "the Doctrine is indeed our

---

[1] Barua & Sinha, *Barhut Inscriptions*, p. 42, f.n. 1.

[2] "*Iti pi so Bhagavā arahaṃ sammā-sambuddho vijjācaraṇa-sampanno sugato loka-vidū anuttaro purisadamma-sārathi satthā deva-manussānaṃ Buddho Bhagavā ti*". *Dīgha*, *II*, *p*. 93.

[3] B. C. Law, *A History of Pāli Literature*, II, pp. 412 ff.

[4] *Dīgha*, II, p. 93.

Refuge now" [1]. For this and other aspects of *Dhamma, vide* Chap. on Dhamma.

Saṅgha, the third of the Triad, includes *Bhikkhu-saṅgha,* and *Bhikkhuṇī-saṅgha.* It really means *Sāvaka-saṅgha* or a fraternity of disciples. *Saṇgha* literally means *samūha* or group. In early Pāli literature, some of the famous teachers of India are mentioned as *saṅghī* (founder of an order), *gaṇī* (having a following) and *gaṇācariyo* (teacher of a group). At the time of the rise of Buddhism, the Vṛjis, Mallas, and other Kṣatriya tribes were known as *Gaṇarājās* or republican chiefs. Even the Śākyas had their *gaṇa* form of administration. A *saṅgha* is a corporate body which is characterised by the uniformity of creed and conduct (*Diṭṭhi-sīlasaṃghātena saṃghāto ti saṃgho*) [2]. *Samaggatā* or internal cohesion constitutes the real life of a Saṅgha as such. The unity of action and commonness of goal characterise its external life. Thus the *saṅgha* stands essentially as a symbol of unity. The Buddha compares the *saṅgha* to an ocean into which all individual rivers ultimately fall, assuming the common name of the ocean. According to the Buddhist 'Mirror of Faith', Saṇgha *par excellence* is composed of all Ariyan disciples who fill eight exalted positions.

---

[1] *Majjhima,* III, p. 9.

[2] *Sumaṅgala-vilāsinī,* I, p. 230; *Paramatthajotikā,* I, p. 20.

CHAPTER II

PĀRAMITĀ

(*Perfection*)

Pāramī[1] is the same term as *Pāramitā*, and both occur side by side in Dhammapāla's commentary on the *Cariyāpiṭaka*[2]. So far as later Buddhist literature goes, the bulk of Pāli works shows predilection for *pāramī*, and that of Sanskrit works for *pāramitā*. In the Pāli canonical texts, however, *pāramī* is the only form met with. In the *Nidhikaṇḍa-sutta* we have *sāvaka-pāramī*, the perfection of discipleship which is no other than the fruition stage of arhatship, the ripeness of saintship which is the ideal before a Buddhist learner or aspirant. In the *Buddhavaṁsa*, on the other hand, the term *pāramī* is employed as a synonym of *Buddhakarā dhammā*, the virtues or qualities which tend towards making a Budha, i.e., maturing the life of a Bodhisattva for the attainment of Buddhahood in his last birth. Precisely in this sense Dhammapāla uses the term *Buddhakārakā dhammā* and quotes a passage of canonical authority with bearing on the point. The passage cannot be traced in the Pāli Text Society's edition of the *Tipiṭaka*. Even if its antiquity be doubted on this ground (which is not very reasonable), there is the text of the *Buddhavaṁsa* to show that, at least as far back as the 2nd century B.C., *pāramī* was treated as another term for *Buddhakarā* or *Buddhakārakā dhammā*. It goes also to show that already in that time the Pāramīs were counted as ten in Theravāda Buddhism[3], while the prose passage quoted by Dhammapāla clearly speaks of *dasa Buddhakārakā dhammā*.

---

[1] *Pāramī* or *Pāramitā* means 'perfection', 'completeness' or 'highest state'.
[2] *Cariyāpiṭakaṭṭhakathā*, Ceylonese ed., p. 7: *Buddhaguṇānaṁ hetubhāūt Buddhakārakadhammā pāramiyo . . . . pāramitā paripācitā*.
[3] This is clearly implied in counting *mettā* as the 9th *pāramī* (*navamaṁ mettā-pāramīṁ*) and closing the enumeration with *upekkhā* occurring after *mettā*.

The quotations from the *Cariyāpiṭaka*, the *Jātaka-nidāna-kathā* and the *Cariyāpiṭaka* commentary presuppose a Canonical text compared with which the P.T.S. edition appears to be incomplete. These quotations fully attest that ten were the *Pāramīs* recognized in *Theravāda* Buddhism when the *Cariyāpiṭaka* was compiled and taken into the corpus of the Pāli Canon along with and as an adjunct to the *Buddhavaṁsa*. Thus any surmise or conclusion drawn on the basis of the incomplete text of the *Cariyāpiṭaka* regarding the number of *Pāramīs* is apt to be misleading.

These considerations may warrant the statement that when the conception of *Pāramitā* developed in Buddhalogy, the *Theravāda* school counted the *Pāramīs* as ten, while in the Sanskrit works belonging mostly to the *Sarvāstivāda school*, the *Pāramīs* are counted as six.

The ten *Pāramīs*, as enumerated in *Theravāda* are: *dāna* (almsgiving), *sīla* (morality), *nekkhamma* (renunciation), *paññā* (wisdom), *viriya* (energy), *khanti* (forbearance), *sacca* (truth), *adhiṭṭhāna* (resolution), *mettā* (friendliness), and *upekkhā* (indifference). Each of them is practised in three degrees of intensity. And the six *Pāramitās* as recognized in Buddhist Sanskrit tradition, are: *dāna*, *śīla*, *kṣānti*, *vīrya*, *dhyāna*, and *prajñā*. In order to get ten *pāramitās*, the following four are to be added, viz., *upāya*, *praṇidhāna*, *bala* and *jñāna*. A Bodhisattva who has conceived an inspiration to become a Buddha, advances in birth after birth, to higher and higher sanctity, in the practice of the ten perfections until at last he is born as the Buddha preaching the Law and passing away into the everlasting stillness of *Nirvāṇa*, as we find in the *Jātakas*. An exactly accomplished Buddha should acquire all these *pāramitās*. Each of these *pāramītās* may be sub-divided into (1) the ordinary, (2) the inferior, and (3) the unlimited perfection of the virtue. Childers is right in agreement with Clough in saying that *dānapāramitā* expresses the duty in general terms and signifies acts of charity or making offerings without any reference to their nature or value (*vide* Childers' Dict., p. 335). A Bodhisattva after having exercised the ten *pāramītās* in all the three degrees of their intensity, in anterior births, was destined to become an omniscient Buddha. Thus we see that the attainment of Buddhahood is the consequence of the vast accumulation of merit in course of the exercise of the *pāramitās* in previous births. In order to attain Bodhi or enlightenment a Bodhisattva had to fulfil the ten *pāramitās*. He had to undergo several births to fulfil each *pāramitā*. In the *Jātakanidānakathā* we read that these ten *pāramitās* are the *Buddhakārakādhammā*, i.e., the precepts which make one Buddha. The great Śākya prince Siddhārtha before attaining Bodhi found these *pāramitās* out to be the only means of attaining Buddhahood. All the previous Buddhas also had to fulfil them in order to attain Buddhahood. Siddhārtha performed these *pāramitās*. Bodhisattva Sumedha fulfilled *dāna-pāramitā* by giving in charity all the worldly things and his own life; he fulfilled *sīla-pāramitā* by observing precepts and without taking the least care for his own life; he fulfilled *nekkhamma-pāramitā* by renouncing household life like a prisoner always anxious to be released from the prison; he fulfilled *paññā-pāramitā* by learning whatever he could learn from anybody; he fulfilled *viriya-pāramitā* by behaving like a lion, the king of beasts; he fulfilled *khanti-pāramitā* by forbearing all the vicissitudes of life most patiently like the earth; he fulfilled *sacca-pāramitā* by not telling lies for fear of punishment or for temptation or even for the falling of thunder on his head; he fulfilled *adhiṭṭhāna-pāramitā* by steadfastly adhering to his endeavour to become a Buddha like a mountain unmoved by storm coming from all directions; he fulfilled *mettā-pāramitā* by cherishing love and friendliness towards his friends and foes alike like water cooling both the virtuous and the sinner; he fulfilled *upekkhā-pāramitā* by being indifferent to happiness and suffering, like the earth (cf. *Jātaka-nidānakathā*, Vol. 1).

A Buddha is called *Dhammakāya* because he is the embodiment of these ten *pāramitās*. Dr. Barnett points out that *dāna-pāramitā* is not an actual deliverance of the world from poverty but an intention for such deliverance; it is a grace of the spirit. Thus purity of the will is the greatest of all virtues, and the foundation of all. He further points out that *sīla pāramitā* consists essentially in the will to hurt no living creature (vide the Path of Light, Wisdom of the East Series, p. 98).

As for examples of *dāna pāramitā*, we may refer to the following in the *Cariyāpiṭaka*: — *Akitticariyaṁ* (*Akitti Jātaka*, *Jātaka*, Vol. IV), *Saṅkhacariyaṁ* (*Saṅkhapāla Jātaka*, *Jātaka*, Vol. V), *Kurudhammacariyaṁ* (*Kurudhamma Jātaka*, *Jātaka*, Vol. II), *Mahāsudas-*

sanacariyaṁ (*Mahāsudassana Jātaka*, *Jātaka*, Vol. I), *Mahāgovindacariyaṁ* (*Mahāgovinda Suttanta*, *Dīgha Nikāya*, Vol. II), *Nimirājacariyaṁ* (*Nimi Jātaka*, *Jātaka*, Vol. VI), *Candakumāracariyaṁ* (*Khaṇḍahāla Jātaka*, *Jātaka*, Vol. VI), *Sivirājacariyaṁ* (*Sivi Jātaka*, *Jātaka*, Vol. IV), *Vessantaracariyaṁ* (*Vessantara Jātaka*, *Jātaka*, Vol. VI), and *Sasapaṇḍitacariyaṁ* (*Sasa Jātaka*, *Jātaka*, Vol. III). The following are the instances of *sīla-pāramitā* mentioned in the *Cariyāpiṭaka*: —

Sīlavanāgacariyaṁ (*Sīlavanāga Jātaka*, *Jātaka*, Vol. I), *Bhūridattacariyaṁ* (*Bhūridatta Jātaka*, *Jātaka*, Vol. II), *Campeyyanāgacariyaṁ* (*Campeyya Jātaka*, *Jātaka*, Vol. IV), *Cūḷabodhicariyaṁ* (*Cullabodhi Jātaka*, *Jātaka*, Vol. IV), *Mahiṁsarājacariyaṁ* (*Mahisa Jātaka*, *Jātaka*, Vol. II), *Rururājacariyaṁ* (*Ruru Jātaka*, *Jātaka*, Vol. IV), *Mātaṅgacariyaṁ* (*Mātaṅga Jātaka*, *Jātaka*, Vol. IV), *Dhammādhammadevaputtacariyaṁ* (*Dhamma Jātaka*, *Jātaka*, Vol. IV), *Jayaddisacariyaṁ* (*Jayaddisa Jātaka*, *Jātaka*, Vol. V), and *Saṅkhapālacariyaṁ* (*Saṅkhapāla Jātaka*, *Jātaka*, Vol. V).

The examples of *Nekkhamma-pāramitā* can be found in the *Yudhañjayacariyaṁ* (*Yuvañjaya Jātaka*, *Jātaka*, Vol. IV), *Somanassacariyaṁ* (*Somanassa Jātaka*, *Jātaka*, Vol. IV), *Ayoghacariyaṁ* (*Ayoghara Jātaka*, *Jātaka*, Vol. IV), *Bhisacariyaṁ* (*Bhisa Jātaka*, *Jātaka*, Vol. IV), *Soṇapaṇḍitacariyaṁ* (*Soṇananda Jātaka*, *Jātaka*, Vol. V). In the *Cariyāpiṭaka* only one instance of *adhiṭṭhāna-pāramitā* is traceable in the *Temiyacariya*[11] which corresponds to the *Temiya Jātaka* (*Jātaka*, VI) which is also known as the *Mūgapakkha Jātaka* found in the *Jātaka*, Vol. II. As for examples of *sacca pāramitā*, we may cite the following: —

Kapirājacariyaṁ (*Kapi Jātaka*, *Jātaka*, Vol. II), *Saccasavhayapaṇḍitacariyaṁ* (*Saccaṅkira Jātaka*, *Jātaka*, Vol. I), *Vaṭṭapotakacariyaṁ* (*Vaṭṭa Jātaka*, *Jātaka*, Vol. I), *Maccharājacariyaṁ* (*Maccha Jātaka*, *Jātaka*, Vol. I), *Kaṇhadīpāyanacariyaṁ* (*Kaṇhadīpāyana Jātaka*, *Jātaka*, Vol. IV), and *Sutasomacariyaṁ* (*Mahāsutasoma Jātaka*, *Jātaka*, Vol. V). *Mahālomahaṁsacariyaṁ* of the *Cariyāpiṭaka* which corresponds to the *Lomahaṁsa Jātaka* in *Jātaka* Vol. I, is the only instance of *Upekkhā-pāramitā*. *Suvaṇṇasāmacariyaṁ* (*Sāma Jātaka*, *Jātaka*, Vol. VI) and *Ekarājacariyaṁ* (*Ekarāja Jātaka Jātaka*, Vol. III) are the instances of *Mettā-pāramitā* as found in the *Cariyāpiṭaka*. The *Cariyāpiṭaka* is the only work of the Pāli

Canon in which a brief and systematic account of Buddhist *pāramitā* is given, although references are found scattered here and there in the *Pāli Nikāyas*.

The Mahāyāna Buddhist texts are replete with information regarding the fulfilment of *pāramitās* by the Bodhisattva. In the *Śraddhotpādasūtra*, Aśvaghoṣa points out that the Bodhisattvas know that the nature of the *dharma* is the perfection of spotless charity, and they being free from covetousness, practise *dāna pāramitā*. They know that the nature of the *dharma*, being free from the influence of five sensual pleasures, and being free from immorality, is the perfection of stainless morality, and they being far above all these vices, practise *sīla-pāramitā*. They know that the nature of the *dharma* is the perfection of stainless patience, and they being free from malice, practise *khanti-pāramitā*. They know that the nature of the *dharma* is the perfection of pure energy, they being free from indolence, practise *viriya pāramitā*. They know that the nature of the *dharma* having nothing to do with disturbance and confusion, is the perfection of pure tranquillisation, they practise *dhyāna-pāramitā*. They know that the nature of the *dharma* is the perfection of pure wisdom; they being free from darkness of ignorance, practise *prajñā-pāramitā* (cf. The Awakening of Faith in the Mahāyāna by Suzuki, pp. 122—123; vide also outlines of Mahāyāna Buddhism by Suzuki, p. 69).

Thus we see that the *pāramitās* are the excellences of a Bodhisattva who never gets tired of practising the ten virtues of perfection. A Bodhisattva in order to obtain Bodhi or enlightenment has to fulfil ten *pāramīs* (*pāramitās*). The *Jātakamālā* [1], the *Mahāvastu* [2], and the *Avadānakalpalatā* [3] contain instances of *pāramitās*. The idea of *pāramitā* is similar according to Northern and Southern Schools of Buddhism with slight variations as noticed above.

We may agree with Dr. Barua in thinking that the Pāramitā doctrine had its root in the age-old Indian conception of faith (*saddhā*), particularly as developed in a *Sutta* of the *Majjhima-*

[1] It contains 35 birth-stories, ten of which have the same titles as those of the *Cariyāpiṭaka* tales.

[2] e.g. *Vānara Jātaka* and *Mahāgovindacariyaṁ*.

[3] e.g. Stories of *Sivi*, *Sasa*, *Matsya*, *Vaṭṭapotaka*, *Ruru*, and *Sutasoma*.

Nikāya and that, as it is, its main importance lies in its bearing on the problem of evolution of personality, whether of the *Buddha* type, or of the *Sāvaka*, or of the *Paccekabuddha* [1]. The Pāli book entitled *Apadāna* contains copious illustrations of how the Sāvaka-pāramī was attained by a large number of men and women as the ripe result of their age-long efforts. In heightening the importance of the moral excellence of Buddhist personalities, the doctrine had necessarily to lay stress on the prolonged character of strivings, and in doing so, it destroyed the belief in the immediate prospects held out by Gotama and transferred the possibility of final fruition to an indefinitely long date [2].

---

[1] B. M. Barua's '*Faith in Buddhism*' (Law's *Buddhistic Studies*, pp. 329 ff.) and '*Mahāyāna in the Making*' (*Proceedings of the Second Oriental Conference*)

[2] Burua's '*Mahāyāna in the Making*' (*Proceedings of the Second Oriental. Conference*).

CHAPTER III

JĀTI

(*Caste*)

Jāti is the generally accepted Indian term to denote caste. *Varṇa* is another term to denote the same. In Pali we meet with the term *Jātivibhaṅga* or *Jātibheda* used in the sense of caste distinction. But the term *Jātivāda* is used to signify the tradition built up by a family or a race or a school. The problem of caste was approached by the Buddhists from three different points of view: — (1) biological (2) occupational and (3) cultural. (1) As a biological term *Jāti* conveys the same meaning as *nikāya* or genus. The main criterion of genera is that they are mutually exclusive, in the sense that sexual union for the purpose of procreation is not possible between them. Each genus consists of a number of species bearing some common characteristics e.g. the two main divisions of the genus plant are represented by grass (*tiṇa*) and trees (*rukkha*). The difference between grasses and trees lies in the fact that the former are pithless within and are pithy without (*antopheggūni bahisārāni*, *Sutta Nipāta Commy*, II, p. 464) and the latter are just the opposite (*bahipheggū antosārā*). The palm trees, cocoanut trees and the rest judged by the above characteristics come under the class grass. The insects, the flies, the ants form three different genera while the hare, the cat, and the rest form a class by themselves. The genus bird too may be thus shown to consist of various species. The similarity of bodily forms, habit of life and the like is a common characteristic of the species belonging to the same genus. If this be applied as a test of difference of genera among men, the Buddhists argue that human beings cannot be taken to represent any more than one species as between a brahmin and a member of any other caste; there is absolutely no difference to be noticed in respect of bodily forms (*Sutta N.* verses 608—611) the habit of life and the rest. Further, sexual union for the purpose of procreation is possible between any two human beings, if they are male and female. The upshot of the biological argument employed by the Buddhists is that the Brahmins, the Kṣatriyas, the Vaiśyas and the Śūdras do not represent *jāti* in the sense of species. They all belong to one and the same species. Thus according to the Buddhists, it cannot be maintained that a brahmin is a brahmin by birth. It is claimed that if both father and mother be persons of high social status, and both of them be persons of high moral character, the progeny born of them will be of a higher type of human beings. The Buddhists hold that the accidence of birth cannot invariably determine the quality or potentiality of the progeny. A brahmin is a brahmin by qualities and not by accidence of birth. ("*Evaṁ sante na jātiyā brāhmaṇo, guṇehi pana brāhmaṇo hoti*" *Sutta N. Commy*, II, 464—466).

(2) Failing to establish caste distinction (*Jātibheda*) on a biological ground the Buddhists proceed to discuss whether and how far the distinction can be justified on occupational ground.

With them the distinction mainly rests on a difference in occupations of life. He who among men lives by cultivation is a cultivator; he who lives by handicraft is an artisan, he who lives by trade is a trader, he who lives by earning wages is a labourer, he who lives by theft is a thief, he who lives by waging war is a warrior, he who lives by acting as a *purohita* is a priest and he who lives by governing a kingdom is a king. (*Sutta Nipāta*, verses 612—619) [1]. Thus the position taken up by the Buddhists may be reduced to

---

[1] Yo hi koci manussesu gorakkhaṃ upajīvati,
evaṃ Vāseṭṭha jānāhi, kassako so, na brāhmaṇo.
Yo hi koci manussesu puthu sippena jīvati,
evaṃ Vāseṭṭha jānāhi, sippiko so, na brāhmaṇo.
Yo hi koci manussesu vohāraṃ upajīvati,
evaṃ Vāseṭṭha jānāhi, vāṇijo so, na brāhmaṇo.
Yo hi koci manussesu parapessena jīvati,
evaṃ Vāseṭṭha jānāhi, pessiko so, na brāhmaṇo.
Yo hi koci manussesu adinnam upajīvati,
evaṃ Vāseṭṭha jānāhi, coro eso, na brāhmaṇo.
Yo hi koci manussesu issattham upajīvati,
evaṃ Vāseṭṭha jānāhi, yodhājīvo, na brāhmaṇo.
Yo hi koci manussesu porohiccena jīvati,
evaṃ Vāseṭṭha jānāhi, yājako so, na brāhmano.
Yo hi koci manussesu gāmaṃ raṭṭhañ ca bhuñjati,
evaṃ Vāseṭṭha jānāhi, rājā eso, na brāhmaṇo.

this that the social status of a person is determined and determinable by means of occupation or livelihood (*Kammanā*).

(3) *Jāti* as a cultural term is entertained by the Buddhists as a mainstay of man's virtue. *Jāti* as an arrogant feeling which impels a man to look down upon other fellow beings is severely criticised but *jāti* as a moral or cultural tradition is highly valued. Each class of men by following a course of good conduct builds up a tradition for itself which has a high value in life as an incentive to betterment of the race and as a check to moral degradation. The tradition awakens in men self-consciousness which is essential to moral progress. The defiance of the cultural tradition thus built up leads to man's fall. (*Jātivādaṁ niraṁkatvā kāmānaṁ vasam upāgamuṁ* — *Sutta Nipāta*, verse 315).

With the Buddhists *Jāti* was also a term to denote the moral disposition of a person. The Ājīvikas divided human beings into six main types according to six such dispositions, each disposition being expressed in terms of a colour: *Kaṇhābhijāti* (of a black disposition), *Lohitābhijāti* (of a red disposition), *haliddābhijāti* [1] (of a yellow disposition), and the like. The *Mahābhārata* substitutes *varṇa* for *abhijāti*, the Pali *saḷābhijātiyo* being the same expression as the Sanskrit *ṣaṭjīvavarṇāh*. The word *jātiko* is used in Pali in the sense of *sabhāvo: uhuṁkajātiko* signifying a person of a boisterous nature. In the Edicts of Asoka the word *jāta* has been used precisely in the sense of moral trait or disposition: "These traits be not mine — is to be wished for (*ete jātā no huvevu mamāti*)" — Separate Rock Edict no. I. Envy, quick loss of temper, cruelty, impatience, want of application, laziness and lethargy are mentioned as specific examples of such *jātas*. Going by this text the abiding moral trait or disposition is the real determining factor of racial or personal type.

With the Brahmanists, the caste system is of a divine origin. It devolved as though from the very beginning of creation out of the created form of *Nārāyaṇa* himself. According to the Buddhist *Agañña suttanta*, the entire social order including the state and the

---

[1] *Aṅguttara Nikāya*, III, p. 384.

caste divisions developed gradually among men according to social needs. The *sutta* repudiates the divine origin of both the state and social order. According to this Buddhist *sutta* the caste distinctions had originated in differences in occupations or means of livelihood. In other words, it is the class which afterwards hardened into caste. All the arguments of the Buddhists against the Brahmanic theory of caste which lie scattered in different Pāli *suttas* have been summed up in the concluding chapter of the *Divyāvadāna* (Chap. 33). The *Divyāvadāna* opines: Just as thoughtless children while playing about on a high road heap up dust and sand in different shapes and christened them saying "this is milk, this is curd, this is meat and this is ghee," just so stand the four *Varṇas* as expounded by the Brahmins [1].

The arguments in the *Vāseṭṭha sutta* are re-stated more effectually in the *Divyāvadāna*. The biological classification of living beings according to genera and species (*liṅga* and *jāti*) may be made and maintained on the ground of similarity or difference in bodily forms, habit and other characteristics, but the application of biological test cannot be established that human beings belong to species more than one. As a matter of fact there is one species among men, all of them possessing common characteristics (*ekaiva jātir loke' smin sāmānyā na pṛithagvidhā, Divyāvadāna* p. 625). The Brāhmaṇas, the Kṣatriyas, the Vaiśyas and the Śūdras are all names arbitrarily fixed. A name so fixed has no especial connotation of its own. Suppose four sons are born in a family and their father chooses to call one *Nandaka* (gladdener), one *Jīvaka* (the living), one *Aśoka* (sorrowless) and one *Śatāyu* (the long-lived). It cannot be deduced from these names that one who is called *Nandaka* is actually the person who gladdens, one who is called *Jīvaka* is actually the person who lives, one who is called *Aśoka* is actually the person who is free from sorrow, and one who is called *Śatāyu* is actually the person who lives a hundred years. There are certain distinctive moral, intellectual or occupational traits acquired or developed by

[1] "*Yathā hi dārakā bālāḥ krīḍamānā mahāpathe*
pāṁśupuñjāni saṁpiṇḍya svayaṁ nāmāni kurvate
idaṁ kshīram idaṁ dadhi idaṁ māṁsam idaṁ ghṛitam
na ca bālasya vacanāt pāṁśavo 'nnaṁ bhavanti hi
varṇās tathaiva catvāro yathā brāhmaṇa bhāshase" (*Divyāvadāna, p.* 626).

different persons as they grow up in life but these distinctive traits cannot be predicated of persons because of their birth in a certain home and by the union of certain parents. (*Divyāvadāna*, pp. 629—630). The differences that exist among men are primarily individual in character. The degree of difference in moral, intellectual, and occupational qualities which may be shown to exist between a so-called Brahmin and a so-called *śūdra*, may equally be shown to exist between two sons born of the same parents. According to time-honoured customs of India a Brahmin is allowed to marry from all the four castes, a *kṣatriya* from three, a *vaiśya* from two and a *śūdra* from one only which is his own caste. Thus a Brahmin may be the father of four sons by his four wives from different castes, the son gaining the social status of his mother. There is no invariable law that given equal chances the son by the Brahmin mother will excel one born by the *sūdra* mother. The status of the four sons is determined arbitrarily.

It is claimed that the Brahmin is generated from the mouth of Brahmā, the *Kṣatriya* from the thigh, the *Vaiśya* from the navel, and the *Śūdra* from the feet. This is only an allegory which is not suggestive of any congenital difference between a Brahmin and a *Kṣatriya*, between a *Kṣatriya* and a *Vaiśya* or between a *Vaiśya* and a *Śūdra*. The allegory rather suggests that the difference had originated in the difference in the training and occupation. That is to say, it is the *karma* which determines the difference among men in social status. There is no such certitude that a Brahmin will be reborn after his death in the *brahmaloka* because he is a Brahmin and a *Śūdra* will be reborn in a lower world because he is a *Śūdra*. The destiny of each person is individually determined by his good or bad deeds.

At the time of the Buddha Gautama there were four classes of the people, viz., *Khattiyas*, *Brāhmaṇas*, *Vessas and Suddas*. They were known as *cattāro vaṇṇā* or the four castes. *Vaṇṇa* literally means colour; some translate it as appearance. In the Buddhist books [1], *Khattiyas* have been given preference over the *Brāhmaṇas*, whereas in the Brahmin literature the *Brāhmaṇas* occupy the first place. The *Upanishads* speak of the *Khattiya* superiority, and in the

[1] Cf. *Ambaṭṭha Sutta*, *D.N.*, I; *Aggañña Sutta*, of *D.N.*, III; *Lalitavistara*, ch. III.

Chāndogya the superior learning of the *Khattiyas* is frequently referred to. Of these four castes, the *Khattiyas* and the *Brāhmaṇas* have been given precedence in salutation, homage, obeisance and the due ministry [1]. The Buddha did not lay much stress on the caste distinctions, which, he said, were unscientific. In the *Ambaṭṭha Sutta* the Buddha is said to have refuted the charge of Ambaṭṭha by saying that the *Śākyas*, among whom he was born, were not menials but *Khattiyas*, and that *Ambaṭṭha*, a *Kaṇhāyana Brāhmaṇa*, was a descendant of a slave girl. Moreover, he tried to prove that the *Khattiyas* were superior to the *Brāhmaṇas*.

Khattiya is the lord of the fields. This term means a „*Rājā*" which is taken in the sense of a nobleman. There are good and bad nobles. A bad noble deprives a living being of life, is a thief, is unchaste, speaks lies, slanders, uses rough words, is greedy, malevolent, and holds wrong views. A good noble, on the other hand, abstains from murder, theft, unchastity, lying, slandering, gossiping, greed, malevolence and false opinions (*Aggañña Suttanta, Dīgha N*). It is distinctly stated that the *Khattiyas* are the best of the four classes (cf., *Majjhima Nikāya*, I, 358; *SN*. I, 153, II, 284 and *Aggañña Sutta*) [2]. A son born of a Brahmin maiden by a *Kṣatriya* youth was eligible for receiving seat and water as tokens of great respect from the *Brāhmaṇas*, for partaking of the feast offered to the dead or of the food boiled in milk, or of the offerings to gods, or of the food sent as a present, for learning the sacred verses of the *Brāhmaṇas* and marrying *Brāhmaṇa* girls. But he was not allowed to receive the consecration ceremony of a *Kṣatriya* because he was not of pure descent on his mother's side. The same privileges could also be enjoyed by one born of a *Kṣatriya* maiden by a *Brāhmaṇa* youth (*Ambaṭṭha Sutta, Dīgha N.I.*). It should be noted that if a *Kṣatriya* was outlawed by other *Kṣatriyas*, he was eligible for enjoying all the privileges mentioned above from the hands of the *Brāhmaṇas*. So we find that even when a *Kṣatriya* had fallen into

[1] *Majjhima Nikāya, Sutta no. 90. — Cattāro 'me, mahārāja, vaṇṇā—Khattiyā, Brāhmaṇā, Vessā, Suddā. Imesaṁ kho, mahārāja, catunnaṁ vaṇṇānaṁ dve vaṇṇā aggam akkhāyanti—khattiyā ca brāhmaṇā ca, yadidam abhivādanapaccuṭṭhānañjalikammasāmīcikamman ti.*

[2] *"Khattiyo seṭṭho jane tasmim ye gottapaṭisārino, vijjācaraṅasampanno so seṭṭho devamānuse".*

the deepest degradation, it held good that the *Kṣatriyas* were superior and the *Brāhmaṇas* inferior (Cf. *Majjhima Nikāya* I, 358).

Next we take up the case of the Brahmins who were proud of their caste. It happened that a Brahmin, out of homage, partook of the leavings of food from the man of the lowest caste, but as soon as he had eaten, he thought that he had disgraced his birth, his clan, and his family, because he had taken the leavings of a churl. His remorse was so very keen that he plunged into the jungle not to show his face to the human world, where he died forlorn. (*Jāt.*, II, 57).

The Brahmins were so very proud of their caste that in one instance we find that a Brahmin when he grew old, said to his son thus: "Don't let my body be burnt in a cemetery where any outcaste can be burnt, but find some uncontaminated place to burn me in." (*Jāt.*, Cowell, II, 37).

The Pāli literature mentions the following kinds of *Brāhmaṇas*: (1) *Udiccadesa Brāhmaṇas*, i.e., Brahmins who lived in the Northern of North-western country (*Jāt*, I, 178, 216, 240, 263); (2) *Kāsī Brāhmaṇas*, i.e., Brahmins who lived at *Kāsī*. (*Jāt.* II, 50, 59, 115); (3) *Brāhmaṇas of Rājagaha and Magadha* who were very superstitious, holding false views and believing in luck. (*Jāt.* I, 215); (4) *Brāhmaṇas of Bhāradvāja Gotta* (*Vide Tevijja Sutta, Dīgha Nikāya*, I), and (5) *Kaṇhāyana Brāhmaṇas* [1]. It is one of the famous sayings of the Buddhists: —

"Foremost in virtue were the men of old,
Those brahmins who remembered ancient rules.
In them well-guarded were the doors of sense.
They had achieved the mastery of wrath.
In meditation and the Norm they took delight,
Those brahmins who remembered ancient rules."

(*S.N.*; *Saḷāyatana-vagga*: "*Book of the Kindred Sayings*," IV, p. 74).

Brahmins in name there were many; but real Brahmins could hardly be found. The *Jātaka* relates a story of the dearth of good and real Brāhmaṇas (*Jāt.*, Cowell, IV, 227). In it is given a descrip-

[1] *Mantānam kattāro, mantānam pavattāro* = makers of *mantras* and repeaters of *mantras*. *Digha*, I, 239.

tion of ten kinds of Brahmins who have lost their Brahminhood.

A true Brahmin is one who has removed all sinfulness, who is free from haughtiness, impurity, and greed; who is an accomplished master of the Veda, and has fulfilled the duties of holiness (*Vinaya Texts*, p. 79, S.B.E., XIII, *Mahāvagga*, 1st *Khandha*). He eats only one meal of rice a day, and he never touches strong drink (*Jāt.* IV, 230). Besides, he must be a repeater of the sacred words, knowing the mystic verses by heart, and he must have acquired the three Vedas with the indices, the ritual, phonology and the exegesis and the legend; be learned in the idioms and grammar, versed in *lokāyata* reasoning, and in the theory relating to the signs of the body of a great man (*Ambaṭṭha Suttanta, Dīgha N.* I, *Soṇadaṇḍa Sutta, Dīgha*, I, p. 120; Cf., *A.N.* I, 163; *Divyāvadāna*, 620, etc.)[1]. In order to be a real *Brāhmaṇa* one must have five things. In the first place he must be of pure birth and descent; secondly, he must know the threefold Vedic lore. He must be an accomplished master of all Vedic *mantras* (*Dīpavaṃsa*, 5, 61—71), and be proficient in allied branches of Brahmanical learning; thirdly, he must have handsome and pleasant appearance and fair colour; fourthly, he must be virtuous, and lastly, he must be learned and wise (*Soṇadaṇḍa Sutta*: *Dīgha* I). Buddha said in one of the *suttas* of the *Dīgha Nikāya*[2] that wisdom (*paññā*) and conduct (*sīla*) are necessary for constituting a true Brahmin (Cf., *Soṇadaṇḍa Sutta*). We may call one a Brāhmaṇa who is thoughtful, blameless, settled and dutiful. One should not attack a Brāhmaṇa, but no Brāhmaṇa should let himself fly at his aggressor. He should not offend others by body, word or thought. One does not become a Brāhmaṇa by his plaited hair. He in whom there are truth and righteousness is a Brāhmaṇa. A Brāhmaṇa should meditate in a forest and must be free from bonds and attachments. He should endure reproach and know the end of his suffering. He should avoid life-slaughter. He must be tolerant to the intolerant, mild with the violent, and free from

---

[1] "*Ajjhāyako mantadharo tiṇṇaṃ vedānaṃ pāragū saṇighaṇḍuketubhānaṃ sākkharappabhedānaṃ itihāsapañcamānaṃ padako veyyākaraṇo lokāyatamahāpurisalakkhaṇesu anavayo*".

[2] Wisdom in the sense of that which is the contrary of *avijjā*, ignorance, or ignorance of the action of *Karma*, of the four noble truths and of the doctrine of the *āsavas* or cardinal sins.

greed among the greedy. He must not utter harsh words. He should not foster desire for this world or for the next. He is a Brāhmaṇa who has risen above ties and who is free from sin or impurity. He is pure, serene, undisturbed and bright like the moon. He has abandoned all desires and has conquered all the world. His passions are extinct. He is noble, a hero, a great sage, a conqueror, the accomplished and the awakened. He is perfect in knowledge and he is truly a sage (Vide *Brāhmaṇavagga, Dhammapada*, pp. 50—60, Cf., *Vāseṭṭha Sutta* of the *Sutta Nipāta*, *Brahmāyū Sutta* of the *M.N.*, the *Brāhmaṇa Saṃyutta* of the *S.N.*, the *Jānussoni Sutta* of the *A.N.*, and so forth). A true Brahmin is he who is immune from the assaults of perception and who has no craving to be reborn either here or elsewhere. He dwells with a clear conscience and without any perplexity.

"It is clear," says T. W. Rhys Davids, "that the word Brahmin in the opinion of the early Buddhists conveyed to the minds of the people an exalted meaning, a connotation of real veneration and respect." He further points out that, "If the contention of the Buddhists had been universally accepted, and if the word Brahmin had come to mean, not only a man of a certain descent, but exclusively a man of a certain character and insight, then the present caste system of India could never have grown up." "The social supremacy of the Brāhmaṇs by birth became accepted as an incontrovertible fact and the inflood of popular superstition which overwhelmed the Buddhist movement, overwhelmed also the whole pantheon of the Vedic gods. Buddhism and Brahmanism alike passed practically away, and modern Hinduism arose on the ruins of both." (*Dialogues of the Buddha*, pt. I, pp. 140 sqq.). It is one of the injunctions of the Buddha that every one having certain abilities should be allowed to teach and that if he does teach, he should teach all keeping nothing back and shutting no one out (Introduction to the *Lohicca Sutta*, *ibid.* 285). It appears from this that a teacher belonging to a higher caste would not refuse to teach anybody belonging to an inferior caste. It is interesting to note that the Brahmins at first gave themselves up to meditation. Hence they were called *Jhāyakas*, but some people, being incapable of enduring meditation in forest leaf-huts, engaged themselves in writing books, hence they were called *Ajjhāyakas*, or the repeaters of the Vedas.

The Brahmins had their fivefold code for achieving the ideal. This code consists of: (1) The Truth (*sacca*); (2) Austerities (*tapa*); (3) Chastity (*brahmacariya*); (4) Study (of Vedic lore); and Munificence (*cāga*) — i.e., to the Brahmins. (Lord Chalmers, *Further Dialogues of the Buddha*, I, p. xix).

Service was divided into four by the Brāhmaṇas: service of a Brahmin, of a noble, of a middle class man, and of a peasant. Any member of all four classes might serve a Brahmin. A noble might be served by another noble or by a middle-class man or by a peasant. A middle-class man might be served by another middle-class man or by a peasant, and a peasant might be served only by a peasant. The Buddha refuted this selfish classification of the Brahmins and based his contention on moral and ethical grounds alone. In the opinion of the Buddha, one should not assert that all services are to be rendered or that all services are to be refused. If the service makes one bad and not good, it should not be rendered. But if it makes him better and not worse, then it should be rendered. This is the guiding consideration which should decide the conduct of Brahmins, nobles, middleclass men and peasants. The Buddha further points out that lineage does not enter into a man's living either good or bad. (*Esukārī Sutta* of *M.N.*, *Further Dialogues of the Buddha*, II, p. 100).

It appears from the comparative frequency of the discussions on the matter of Brahmin pretensions, that the subject of caste was a burning problem at the time of the composition of the *Nikāyas*. No other social problem is referred to so often; and the Brahmins would not be so often represented as expressing astonishment or indignation at the position taken up regarding it by the early Buddhists unless there had really been a serious difference on the subject between the two schools. But the difference, though real, has been gravely misunderstood. As Rhys Davids has said: "The disastrous effects, from the ethical, social, and political points of view, of these restrictions and of caste as a whole, have been often grossly exaggerated and the benefits of the system ignored. And we are entirely unwarranted in supposing the system, as it now exists, to have been in existence also at the time when Buddhism arose in the valley of the Ganges. Our knowledge of the actual facts of caste, even as it now exists, is still confused and inaccurate. The theories put forward to explain the facts are loose and irreconcilable"[1]. There was a common phrase current among the people which divided all the world into four *vaṇṇas* (colours or complexions). The priests put themselves first and had a theological legend in support of their contention. But it is clear from the Piṭakas that this was not admitted by the nobles. And it is also clear that no one of these divisions was a caste. There was neither *connubium* nor commensality between all members of one *vaṇṇa*, nor was there a governing council for each.

The fourth was distinguished from the other by social positions. And though in a general rough way the classification corresponded to the actual facts of life, there were insensible gradations within the four classes and the boundary between them was both variable and undefined. The theory of caste, or *Jāti*, easily breaks down when we see that a Brahmin and a *Caṇḍāla* do not differ from their physical constitution and can procreate children.

Mahākaccāna was asked by King Avantiputta of Madhurā as to the Brahmanical claim that the Brahmins were superior to all other castes. The king said, "The Brahmins maintain that they alone form the superior class, all other classes being inferior. The Brahmins alone form the white class, all other classes being black. That purity resides in Brahmins alone and not in non-Brahmins, and that Brahmins are Brahmā's legitimate sons born from his mouth, offsprings of his, creations of his, and his heirs". Kaccāna convinced him of the equal footing of all the four classes, inasmuch as any member of the four classes could, when he had grown rich and wealthy, employ any member of any of the other three classes as servants.

The emptiness of the Brahmin claim to superiority is shown by the fact that if any one, be he a noble, Brahmin, Vessa or Sudda, kills, robs, lies, slanders, covets, harbours ill-will, is of bitter tongue, or has a wrong outlook, he after death must pass to a state of misery or woe, or to purgatory. The same misery awaits each one who is guilty of such crimes. It is also demonstrated by the fact that if any one, be he a noble, a middle-class man or a peasant, abstains from the crimes noted above, he passes after death to bliss and

---

[1] *Dialogues of the Buddha*, pt. I, pp. 96—97.

heaven. It can further be proved by the fact that if any one, be he a Brahmin, a noble, a middle-class man or a peasant, is a burglar, thief or house-breaker, he is equally punished by the ruler of the realm, irrespective of the caste of the accused. It is also apparent from the fact that he, whether Brahmin, Vessa, or Sūdda, who cuts off his hair and beard, and dons the yellow robes and goes from house to house as a pilgrim, abstaining from killing, stealing and lying, eating but one meal a day and living the higher life in virtue and goodness; such a one is honoured and respected and provided with all the necessities of life. (*Madhura Sutta* of the *Majjhima Nikāya*, II, pp. 83—90; cp. *Assalāyana Sutta, M.N.*, II, pp. 147 foll., and *Esukārī Sutta, M.N.*, II, pp. 177 foll., where the Brahmin pretentions are also discussed). Thus we find that the *Madhura Sutta* deals with caste system under five heads. It teaches that caste cannot ensure material success in life, cannot save the wicked from punishment hereafter, cannot debar the good from bliss hereafter, cannot shield the evil-doers from criminal law, and cannot affect the uniform veneration extended to the monk, whether be he sprung from the highest or the lowest of the four castes. In all those important respects the four castes are equal. Lord Chalmers is right in pointing out that this *sutta* does not go on to state, nor does any other *sutta* venture to state, that in every possible respect the four castes were on one identical footing of equality. Such a statement would have evinced a certain blindness to facts for, although in all essentials, caste was not an empty name to the Buddha, yet the distinctions of caste had a residual sphere of activity and ranked among the accidents of life. Whilst caste had no part in the higher life, and was irrelevant in the less trivial of mundane relations, yet there undoubtedly remained the region where, in the absence of higher qualifications, the hereditary distinctions of caste were accepted as an appropriate differentia between little men. But into this trivial region Gautama disdained to enter. He was content to explode the caste theory without denouncing it as a formal institution (*Vide J.R.A.S.*, 1894, p. 348)

Brahmin wives of Brāhmaṇas have their periods and they are subject to conception. How then can the Brahmins claim to be born of Brahmā's mouth? In the Yonakamboja and other adjacent countries, there are only two classes, masters and slaves. A master can become a slave and *vice versa*. This does not at all lend any support to the Brahmin's claim. It is clear, therefore, that the caste system of the Brahmins did not prevail in the Yonakamboja region.

Not only a Brahmin, but a man of other three classes can develop in his heart the love that knows no hate or ill. Not only a Brahmin, but a man of other three classes also can go down to the river with his string of red bath balls to shampoo himself and rub off the dust and dirt. The fire kindled by any one of the four classes blazes up with a bright flame and serves the purpose of a fire. When a son is born to a young noble and a Brahmin maiden, he is styled both a noble and a Brahmin; when a son is born to a noble maiden and a young Brahmin, he is styled both a Brahmin and a noble. Between two uterine Brahmin brothers, of whom one is an educated scholar, and the other not educated, Brahmins generally give preference to the educated one in making gifts, but if the educated one is wicked and profligate, and the uneducated one is virtuous, the Brahmins generally give preference to the uneducated man. Therefore, the standard of distinction between *vaṇṇa* and *vaṇṇa* depends on purity and goodness (cp., *Assalāyana Sutta, M.N.*, II, 147—157). Here also we find that the Buddha speaks against the Brahmanical pretentions that the Brahmins are superior to all other castes (cf. also *Caṅkī Sutta*, II, 164—177, where also the Buddha condemns the Brahmanical pretentions as to their superiority).

In the 6th or 5th century B.C. the Brāhmaṇas took up higher occupations to earn their livelihood. They acted as chaplains (*Jātaka*, IV, 188), ministers [1] and courtiers (*Jāt.*, II, 166). The Brahmins also followed such lower professions as hunters (*Jāt.*, II, 14; III, 276), who used to kill many deer and live on them; carpenters (*Jāt.*, IV, 129), who used to bring wood from the forest and make carts; goatherds (*Jāt.* III, 242), and snake-charmers (*Jāt.* IV, 283).

We find many instances of greediness of the Brahmins in Buddhist literature. The Brāhmaṇas thought exultantly of large sums of money and large supplies of food. They sought in the dreams of kings pretexts for sacrifices and personal gain (*Jāt.* I, 187; cf. *Jāt.* I, 255, where the Brāhmaṇas are described as a greedy lot). The

[1] It should be noted that the Kṣatriyas also enjoyed the privilege of being ministers to the king (*Jātaka*, III, 102).

Buddha, while at Jetavana, spoke about a Brahmin retained by the King of Kosala, who had the power of telling which swords were lucky, but who was very greedy. The Brahmin made it a rule only to commend the work of those smiths who gave him presents, while he rejected the work of those who did not bribe him (*Jāt.* I, 277). A Brahmin who was appointed as a judge by the King of Benares was addicted to accepting bribes (*Jāt.* VI, 69).

The Brahmin students, like the Kṣatriyas, were admitted into the University of Taxila. They were, like the Kṣatriyas, taught the three Vedas and various arts (*Jāt.* III, 105).

The Vessas were the trading people. In the Buddhist literature their position was next to the Brāhmaṇas (cf. *Aggañña Sutta, Dīgha Nikāya,* III). They adopted the married state, and set on foot various trades. The Jātakas contain references to such trading people and trading families (cf. *Jāt.* II, 163, 199).

The Suddas come next to the Vessas. They were known in the Buddhist age as slaves as opposed to freemen; children born to such slaves were also slaves. We hear of them quite occasionally as domestic servants in the houses of the rich (*Jāt.* (Fausböll) IV, 200). According to the *Aggañña Sutta,* those who took to hunting and such debasing pursuits were known as Suddas (the lowest grade of folk). *Vāsabhakhattiyā*, a daughter of a slave-girl, who became the consort of the King of Kosala, was degraded, together with her son Viḍūḍabha, because they were of servile rank (*Jāt.* I, 27; and see also *Jāt.* IV, 91). It is interesting to note that the name of a noble family should not be given to a slave-girl's bastard child. It happened that a chaplain fell in love with a slave-girl who conceived and enquired of him as to the name by which the child should be called. The chaplain replied thus, "My dear, here is a tree called *Uddāla,* and you may name the child as *Uddālaka.* It can never be that the name of a noble family should be given to a bastard child of a slave girl" (*Jat.* IV, p. 188).

Besides these four classes there were lower *varṇas,* such as *caṇḍālas, pukkusas, veṇas, nesādas, rathakāras,* potters, weavers, leather-workers, barbers, matmakers, fishermen, drummers (*bherivādaka-kula, Jāt.* I, 146), conchblowers (*saṅkhadhamakakula, Jāt.* I, 147), ploughmen or cultivators (*Jāt.* I, 168), greengrocers, carters, water-carriers, field-labourers (*Jāt.* III, 107), etc. It is true that the *veṇas*, the *nesādas* and the *rathakāras* were undoubtedly aboriginal tribesmen who were hereditary craftsmen. So also in the case of matmakers, potters, weavers, leather-workers, and water-carriers who adopted low occupations from generation to generation; undoubtedly all these were *hīnajātīya*, or low-caste people. In the Buddhist age a barber was rewarded by the King with a village (*Jāt*. I, 30). A true believing barber was allowed to listen to the Master's discourse, and enter the *Saṅgha*. It appears from this that there was no bar for a man of lower *varṇa* to come to listen to the Buddha's *dhamma* (*Jāt*. II, 4).

Mention is made of a *caṇḍāla* village which was inhabited by low-caste *caṇḍālas* only (*Jāt*. IV, 124). There was a belief in Buddha's time that the *caṇḍālas* used to bring bad luck to thoso who saw them (*Jāt*. IV, 235). The *caṇḍālas* had their own manner of speech and their own language. There was a *caṇḍāla* village outside Ujjenī (*Jāt*. IV, 244). The *caṇḍālas* were not admitted into the University of Taxila. Two *caṇḍāla* brothers went to study at Taxila, posing as Brahmins, but when they were found out, they were expelled (*Jāt*. IV, 244). The *caṇḍālas* were so much hated by the Brahmins that some among them on account of having tasted the food of a *caṇḍāla*, were put out of caste (*Jāt*. IV, 235). A *caṇḍāla* is described as having been able to secure, as he wished, the beautiful lady, *Diṭṭhamaṅgalikā*, daughter of a prosperous merchant. The lady was kept in the *caṇḍāla* settlement outside the city without transgressing in any way the rules of caste. A son of this beautiful lady, when he was seven or eight years old, learned the three Vedas, and at sixteen practised charities to the Brahmins (*Jāt*. IV, 235). There is an instance where we find how a wise and learned *caṇḍāla* was badly treated by a *Brāhmaṇa* (*Jāt*. III, 153).

A young Brahmin learnt a charm from a low caste *caṇḍāla*. When once asked by the King as to the name of the teacher from whom he had learnt it, he felt shame to say that he had learnt it from a low-caste *caṇḍāla*, and spoke falsely before the King. Instantly the charm was gone. The Brahmin spoke to the King the truth. Hearing this the King thought within himself, "When one has a treasure so priceless, what has birth to do with it?"

According to the Buddha, people belonging to high or low caste could attain arahatship. There are instances in the Pāli literature where we find that a ploughman or a cultivator attained arahatship (*Jāt.* I, 168); a fisherman's son was admitted into the order and he afterwards won the glory of arahatship (*Jāt.* I, 105). A careful study of the *Theragātha* and its commentary will convince one of the fact that people belonging to different castes, from the highest aristocracy to the lowest scavenger, lived together in fraternal affection and equanimity, and won the highest bliss (*vide* my *History of Pāli Literature*, pp. 500 foll.). Any person belonging to the lower castes, as for example, *caṇḍāla*, was not eligible for kingship. A *caṇḍāla*, simply because he was a *caṇḍāla*, was not made a king. It was distinctly stated that, had he been of a higher caste, he would have been made a king (*Jāt.* III, 18).

At the time of the Buddha we meet with several instances where marriage took place among the candidates of equal rank. A gentleman of a country near Sāvatthī asked in marriage for his son, a young Savatthian girl of equal rank (*Jāt.* I, 124). A Brahmin was married to a bride of his own rank (*Jāt.* I, 292). The daughter of a lay sister at Sāvatthī was married to a husband of the same caste (*Jāt.* I, 294). A Sudda had a beautiful daughter; when she grew up, she was married into a family "as good as her own" (*Jāt.* II, 158). A Brahmin householder of Benares had a son and a daughter; when the son grew up, his father brought a wife home for him from a family of equal rank (*Jāt.* III, 108). There is an example of *asavarṇa* marriage (marriage outside *varṇa* or caste) in the case of the daughter of the chief garland-maker of Sāvatthī, named Mallikā, marrying Pasenadi, the King of Kosala (*Jāt.*, III, 244).

Gahapati, or householder, may be found among the classes already mentioned. In the Pāli literature the word *Kuṭumbika* occurs (*Jāt.* I, 105; *Jāt.* II, 266) which means a landowner (and a country squire). It may refer to a landowner belonging to any caste, but in the case of Brāhmaṇas the term "*Brāhmaṇagahapatikā*", or "Brahmin householders", occurs in several places in Pāli literature; for example: "*Amaccāpi Brāhmaṇagahapatikā pi*" in *Jāt.* I, p. 506 (Fausböll).

CHAPTER IV

ARIYASACCAS

(Four Noble Truths)

In the Theravāda and Sarvāstivāda doctrines, the *Ariyasaccas* or Four Noble Truths are regarded as the quintessence of Buddhism as propounded by the Master himself. It is categorically asserted in the *Peṭakopadesa*[1], that all that was uttered by the Buddha from the day of his enlightement to that of his great decease, all that he propounded in the form of a *sutta* or a *geyya* or a *vyākaraṇa* or a *gāthā* or an *udāna*, all fall within the scope of the Four Noble Truths.

The Sutta which embodies them in their authoritative form is known as the *Dhammacakkapavattana Sutta*. This Sutta is entertained by tradition as *Paṭhama Dhammadesanā* or the very first public statement of Buddha's position as a teacher and thinker. There is little doubt that the text of this discourse is highly important in the history of Buddhism as a definite formulation of Buddha's doctrine from the orthodox point of view. The *Ariyasaccas*, as generally interpreted, consist of the following four items of truth: (1) *Dukkha*, commonly translated as 'suffering', (2) *Dukkha-samudaya*, commonly translated as 'origin of suffering'. (3) *Dukkhanirodha*, 'cessation of suffering', and (4) *Dukkhanirodhagāminī-paṭipadā*, 'the path leading to the cessation of suffering'. Birth, decay, death, sorrow, lamentation, pain, grief and despair are mentioned as common instances of suffering, as generally understood in the world in which we live. Union with persons or things a person does not like or separation from persons or things a person likes is said to be suffering from the mental point of view. To put it in another form, suffering is a painful feeling which arises from getting what one does not desire to get, and not getting what one desires to get[2], in short, from disappointment. The entire position taken

---

[1] *Na kiñci buddhānaṃ bhagavantānaṃ dhammadesanāya dhammacakkato bahiddhā; tassa sabbaṃ suttaṃ ariyadhammesu pariyesitabbaṃ.* Chap. I.

[2] In the texts, the negative statement alone is considered to be sufficient.

up in respect of the first item is reduced to this: "*Saṃkhittena pañcupādānakkhandhā dukkhā*", "the five aggregates of attachment constitute suffering."

In the traditional exposition, each of the terms, birth, death and the rest, is carefully defined. Birth is defined as a particular biological process of development of an individual in a certain species of living beings. Decay is defined as a biological process of infirmity along with the maturity attained by an individual in a particular form of birth. Death is defined as a tragic biological end of an individual in life, resulting from the arrest of vital functions. Sorrow is defined as a mental process of grieving due to the sense of a great loss either of kinsmen or of wealth or of health or of character or of a cherished belief. Lamentation is defined as a verbal expression of sorrow felt in the heart. Pain is defined as bodily uneasiness or discomfort. Misery is nothing but a mental uneasiness or disagreeable feeling. Despair consists in utter dejection of spirit resulting from the sense of great loss beyond recovery. By association is meant contact, coming together, union and mixing with. Further explanation follows which tends to show that birth or decay or death is not in itself suffering. Suffering arises from a sense of disappointment. A person, for instance, wishes: may it be that I shall not be subject to the contingency of birth; but the contingency actually arises in spite of his wishes to the contrary. Thus the question of suffering is inwardly bound up with men's wish or desire in regard to certain things. All such things in connection with which his wish or desire comes into play are summed up by the five aggregates of attachment.

Thus from the consideration of the first item of truth one is led to the second concerning the origin of suffering.

The origin of suffering lies in *Taṇhā*, defined as craving which is potent for rebirth, accompanied by lust and self-indulgence seeking satisfaction now here and now there. There are three kinds of craving: (1) the craving for pleasures of the senses, (2) the craving for becoming and (3) the craving for not-becoming.

From the consideration of the second item, one is left to consider the third concerning the cessation of suffering. The cessation of suffering consists in utter fading away and attenuation of that very craving. *Nirodha* is cessation without any possibility of rebirth.

Craving in its varying forms and various aspects arises in connection with the senses and their respective objects. Where the senses, external and internal, do not come into relation with their objects, craving finds no outlet for self-expression. *Nirodha* is, therefore, that state of the self in which consciousness transcends the sphere of senses and their objects.

If the cessation of suffering is a truth beyond dispute, further question arises: what is the Path leading to the cessation of suffering? This path is called the Noble Eightfold Path. It consists in right view, right resolve, right speech, right action, right livelihood, right effort, right mindfulness, and right concentration. The right view is defined as knowledge in respect of the four items of truth. The right resolve is a resolve to renounce, to get rid of hatred and harming. The right speech consists in abstinence from lying, slandering, use of harsh language and vain talks. The right action consists in abstinence from taking life, stealing and immoral sexual indulgence. The right livelihood consists in following a proper means of existence. The right effort is an honest and earnest effort made to check the rise of immoral states that have not yet arisen, to put a stop to the immoral states that have arisen, to produce the moral states that have not as yet arisen and to preserve and strengthen the moral states that have already arisen. The right mindfulness consists in the practice of the four-fold prescribed mode of *satipaṭṭhāna*. And the right concentration consists in the successful practice of the prescribed mode of *jhāna*.

The formulation of the four truths proceeded on the basis of the doctrine of *Paṭiccasamuppāda* accounting for the origin and cessation of the entire mass of ill. The four truths as formulated in the *Dhammacakkapavattana Sutta* represent a definite procedure or schema of thought. This procedure was not, of course, peculiar to Buddhism. A similar procedure was equally followed in other branches of knowledge, e.g., the Sāṅkhya system of Philosophy, the science of medicine and the science of wealth. "It is not difficult to see", says Kern, "that these four *satyas* are nothing else but the four cardinal articles of Indian medical science, applied to the spiritual healing of mankind, exactly as in the *Yoga* doctrine" [1].

[1] Kern, *Manual of Indian Buddhism*, pp. 46—47, quotes: *Yogasūtra*, II, 15, Comm.: "*yathā cikitsā-Śāstram caturvyūhaṃ: rogo, rogahetur, ārogyaṃ, bhai-*

The term "*dukkha*" is taken in Buddhism in a most comprehensive sense so as to include in it danger, disease, waste and all that constitutes the basis or cause of suffering. In the terminology of one of the earlier thinkers of Buddha's time, *sukha* (pleasure) and *dukkha* (pain) were conceived as two distinct principles, one of attraction, integration or concord and the other of repulsion, disintegration or discord. Considered in this light, *sukha* was taken to be the principle of harmony and *dukkha*, that of discord. In the medical texts *roga* or disease which is just an instance of *dukkha* is defined as that condition of the self, the physical self, when the different organs do not function together in harmony and which are attended with a sense of uneasiness. And *ārogya* or health, the opposite of disease, is defined as that condition of the self when all the organs function together in harmony and are attended with a sense of ease. Thus the problem of *dukkha* is essentially rooted in the feeling of discord or disparity. Birth, decay, or death is not in itself *dukkha* or suffering. These are only a few contingencies in human experience which upset the expectations of men. From the point of view of mind, *dukkha* is just a *vedanā* or feeling which is felt by the mind either in respect of the body or in respect of itself, and as a feeling, it is conditioned by certain circumstances. In the absence of these circumstances there is no possibility of its occurrence. Whether a person is affected by *dukkha* or not depends on the view he takes of things. If the course of common reality be that being once in life, one can not escape either decay or death, and if the process of decay sets in or death actually takes place, there is no reason why that person should be subject to *dukkha* by trying to undo what cannot be undone. Thus *dukkha* is based upon misconstruction of the *dhammatā* or law of things or the way of happening in life. If the order of things cannot be changed, two courses are open to individuals to escape from *dukkha*: (1) to view and accept the order as it is, and (2) to enquire if there is any state of *citta* or consciousness, on attaining to which an individual is no longer affected by the vicissitudes of life.

The Buddhist answer to this enquiry is that there is such a state of consciousness. In this state consciousness becomes unrelated with

---

ṣajyaṃ iti, evam idam api -śāstram caturvyūham eva, tadyathā: saṃsāraḥ, saṃsārahetur, mokṣo, mokṣopāya iti."

anything which is mundane or mental. To reach this state is to be out of touch with the object of every description. *Jhāna* or *samâdhi* is the tried mode of reaching that state of consciousness in this present conscious experience.

Jhāna or *samādhi* is the main point in the Noble Eightfold Path, the remaining seven points being directly or indirectly connected with the last point. The right view and the right resolve representing, as they do, the first two points are nothing but rightly focussing the attention and rightly directing the course of the will. The right speech, the right action and the right livelihood, taken together, are the three points that are concerned with the means of purifying one's conduct, thereby removing obstacles in the path to *samādhi*. The right effort signifies the means of consciously determining the character of the motive in practising *jhāna* or *samādhi*. The right mindfulness represents the tried means of inducing the *jhānik* mood and cultivating mental awareness of all experiences that occur in the course of meditation. A great stress is laid in Buddhism on the perfection of the method of attaining to that free and pure state of consciousness.

It will be noted that *dukkha* is nowhere postulated as a permanent feature of reality. It is admitted and entertained only as a possible contingency in life as it is generally lived. *Nirodha* representing, as it does, the free and pure state of consciousness, is posited as the ultimate nature of reality. The procedure of thought wich has been followed does not admit of the consideration of the question whether Buddhism is pessimism or optimism. Among all the Buddhist sects or schools, the Kukkulikas are said to have taken up a position leading to a pessimistic construction of existence (*sabbe saṃkhārā kukkuḷā*) [1]. But this was not universally accepted by the Buddhists.

[1] *Points of Controversy, Prefatory notes*, p. xlii.

CHAPTER V

ARIYA AṬṬHAṄGIKA MAGGA

(*The Noble Eightfold Path*)

We have seen that in the architectonic of Buddhist thought as represented by the noble truths, the fourth item is the Path leading to the cessation of suffering. This path is called the Noble Eightfold Path — the *Ariya Aṭṭhaṅgika Magga.* This is otherwise called *Majjhimā paṭipadā* or the Middle Path. The Aśokan expression 'majhaṃ paṭipādeyamā ti' (S.R.E.) 'that we will fulfil the mean', enables us to understand that the term *majjhimā paṭipadā*, rendered "Middle Path", is rather a misleading coinage. All that king Aśoka wanted his officials to do was to fulfil the *majjha* or mean, — to realise the ideal of a *via media*. In the expression *Majjhimā-paṭipadā*, on the other hand, *majjhimā* or middle stands as an adjective qualifying *paṭipadā* or path. To explain it in the light of Aśoka's phrase, the Pāli expression must be taken to mean that it is a definite course of thought or of conduct by which the ideal of *Majjha* may be realised. Some such thought developed also in the political thought of Ancient India. According to the earlier opinion, the kings were to carry on their administration on a strict principle, being relentless in method (*ati-tīkṣṇa*). According to the later and more rational opinion, the kings were to follow a principle of polity which is neither too strict nor too lenient (*nātitīkṣṇa, nātimṛdu*). In other words, the political wisdom, according to the later opinion, lay in striking the 'golden mean' between the two extremes. It may now be taken for granted that in many of the Pāli passages the term met with is not *majjhimā* but *majjha*, and that wherever the term *majjha* is introduced, it is introduced as a 'golden mean' between two extremes (*dve antā*). In all these references one may note that *Paṭiccasamuppāda* is mentioned as a formula of thought by which the desired 'mean' can really be fulfilled. Aśoka in his Separate Rock Edict (Dhauli), says "Well propounded is the principle thus: — If any person suffers from arrest or restraint, which eventually ends in imprisonment [1], many other persons become thereby deeply aggrieved. There you must aim at this, namely, that you will 'fulfil the mean'. You are not to proceed under these (immoral) dispositions, envy, distemper, cruelty, impatience, want of application, laziness and lethargy".

The *majjha* aimed at by Aśoka is a 'mean' between these two extremes, of which one is represented by rashness (*āsulopa*) and the other by laziness (*ālasiya*). By *Majjhimā-paṭipadā, majjha* or 'mean' in the *Dhammacakkapavattana-sutta* is sought to be avoided or evaded, in so far as the verbal expression goes; the two extremes being (1) the method of attaining salvation by thoughtless indulgence in the affairs of lust (*kāmesu kāmasukhallikānuyoga*), and (2) the method of attaining salvation by the rigorous practice of self-mortification (*attakilamathānuyoga*). In the doctrine of the Middle Path, the futility of these two methods is sought to be brought out in many ways and in many places. The thoughtless indulgence in the affairs of lust is the way of the common run of men, and the rigorous practice of self-mortification is the traditional way of the extreme type of ascetics.

The first kind of life is illustrated in the *Ariyapariyesana Sutta* [2] by the life lived by the Bodhisatta as prince Siddhārtha. The second kind of life is exemplifed in the *Mahāsīhanāda Sutta* [3] by the life lived by the same Bodhisatta as an *Acelaka* or *Ajīvika* after he had recounced the world.

So far as English phraseology goes, 'golden mean' is just the expression which verbally fits in with the Buddhist *Majjha* or *Madhya*. The Golden mean is 'the middle course between the two extremes, — a wise moderation'. But the golden mean which the Buddhist has aimed at, is reachable by various degrees of approach from two sides. Thatis to say, the conception and formulation of the golden mean in Buddhism became possible after many centuries

[1] Dr. N. Dutt placing undue reliance on Mr. Basu's interpretation of *baṃdhanantikā*, seeks to maintain that Aśoka was against persons leaving the world and becoming monks. But the word "*baṃdhanantikā*" definitely means something which ends in *baṃdhane* and not that which ends it. Cf. *Dukkhā maraṇantikā*, suffering which culminates in death. (*Dīgha*, II, "*ābādhaṃ māraṇantikaṃ*, p. 128).

[2] *Majjhima Nikāja*, I, p. 160.

[3] *Majjhima Nikāya*, I, pp. 68 foll.

of evolution of religious life and thought of India without reference to which its historical significance cannot be truly realised. A suggestion has been recently made that it is not so much by avoidance or evasion of the two extremes as by bringing out in essence the significance of each trodden or proposed path that the Buddhist ideal of the 'golden mean' may be fulfilled. The underlying spirit of this doctrine of the 'golden mean' in Buddhism has been well expressed in the following verse of the *Dhammapada*, verse 141: —

"Na naggacariyā na jaṭā na paṅkā
nānāsakā thaṇḍilasāyikā vā
rajo ca jallaṃ ukkuṭikappadhānaṃ
sodhenti maccaṃ avitiṇṇakaṅkhaṃ".

„Not by nakedness, not by plaited hair, not by dust, not by fasting, not by lying on the bare ground, not by rubbing with dust and not by sitting motionless, one can purify oneself, if one is not free from desire."

This 'golden mean' served as the guiding principle to the whole of the Vinaya discipline, according to which, the life of the Buddhist Holy Order was to be moulded. The desired effect sought to be produced was to shift the emphasis from things external to the purity internal [1]. The Noble Eightfold Path was propounded as a well-tested method of attaining the internal purity of the self.

The first two factors in this method are *sammādiṭṭhi* and *sammāsaṃkappa* commonly rendered 'right view' and 'right resolve'. *Sammādiṭṭhi*, as used in this context, is otherwise called *aviparīta-dassanā* or a view or belief which is not contrary to truth. Here *sammādiṭṭhi* conveys the sense of faith or belief rather than that of any metaphysical view or theory. It is precisely in some such sense that the Jains use the term *sammādaṃsana*. As explained in the Pāli *Sāleyyakasutta*, [2] (p. 288) *sammādiṭṭhi* suggests an article of faith which is contrary to that which was inculcated by Ajitakesakambalī and his followers. This article of faith consists in the acceptance of the belief that there is such a thing as gift, that there is such a thing as sacrifice, that there is such a thing as oblation to fire, that there are such things as results, immediate and remote, of deeds, well-done and ill-done, this world, the other world, mother,

[1] *Majjhima Nikāya*, Vol. I, p. 39; *"sināto attarena sinānena."*
[2] *Majjhima Nikāya*, Vol. I, pp. 285 foll.

father, adventitious birth, and such well-gifted and well accomplished religious teachers who truly declare the nature of this and the other world after having realised it through their higher perception or intuition [1] and *micchādiṭṭhi* suggests an article of faith just contrary to this [2]. There cannot be *sammādiṭṭhi* or right faith unless there is a clear pre-perception of the moral, intellectual or spiritual situation which is going to arise. In other words, *sammādiṭṭhi* is that form of faith which is only a stepping-stone to *paññā* or knowledge. It is the faith or conviction acquired by a Buddhist *sotāpanna* or 'stream-attainer' who is sure to reach the goal. Once you lay hold of the first factor which is *sammādiṭṭhi*, you are sure to arrive at the last factor, namely, *sammāsamādhi* which is right concentration, the approved means of attaining *visuddhi* or purity, and *vimutti* or emancipation. *Sammā-saṃkappa* or right resolve represents just the will-aspect of the Buddhist faith. It consists in right direction of the will towards the goal. Some of the earlier Upaniṣads teach that all that a man earnestly desires to attain, comes to the fulfilment from the very *saṃkalpa* or determination of will (*yaṃ kāmaṃ kāmayate so' asya saṃkalpādeva samuttiṣṭhati tena sampannaḥ mahīyate*).

The next three factors, namely, *sammā-vācā* (right speech), *sammā-kammanto* (right work) and *sammā-ājīva* (right livelihood) constitute the well-tried method of the attainment of moral purity (*sīla-visuddhi*). The moral purity is not to be viewed as an end in itself but only a means to an end and the end in view is no other than cultivation of mental purity (*citta-visuddhi*), which is attainable by means of the remaining three factors, namely, *sammā-vāyāma* (right effort), *sammā-sati* (right mindfulness), and *sammā-samādhi* (right concentration) [3]. Conduct or external behaviour is only an outward expression of the moral states (*cetasikā dhammā*) [4] which constitute man's internal character. Unless that is thoroughly purified by mindfulness, meditation, concentration and introspection, the attempt will be like preventing the future growth of a tree simply by cutting it down on the surface, leaving the roots

[1] *Majjhima Nikāya*, Vol. I, p. 288.
[2] *Ibid.*, p. 287.
[3] *Majjhima*, Vol. I, p. 148.
[4] *Visuddhimagga*, Vol. I, p. 7; *Paṭisambhidāmagga*, I, p. 44.

intact [1]. The moral character which is the very flower of human estate must grow, if it is to grow at all, of itself, from within. And the object of the last three factors in the Buddhist Path is permanently to remove those obstacles and those immoral dispositions, on the one hand, and to induce or produce those healthy conditions of mind, on the other, whereby one can really help the spontaneous growth of moral character from within [2].

The consideration of these three factors will be taken up in details in the chapter on *Jhāna*. Here we may point out that the Noble Eight-fold Path leaves out two important factors without which the Buddhist system of thought is incomplete. In the *Rathavinīta* and a few other *suttas* of the *Majjhima Nikāya*, it is mentioned that *sīla-visuddhi* in itself is useless, if it does not lead to something still better; that *citta-visuddhi* in itself is useless if it does not lead to something better than it; and that *ñāna-visuddhi* or purity of knowledge in itself is useless, if it does not lead to the ultimate end which consists in the attainment of *vimutti* or emancipation. We cannot say precisely in what state of Buddhist thought the number of factors in the Path was fixed as eight. There is an enumeration, e.g., in the *Saṅgīti suttanta* which expressly recognises two additional factors, namely, *sammā-ñāṇa* or right knowledge and *sammā-vimutti* or right emancipation [3].

---

[1] *Dhammapada*, verse: 338 "*yathāpi mūle anupaddave daḷhe, chinno pi rukkho punar eva rūhati* ....

[2] *Digha*, III, p. 221: *anuppannānaṃ pāpakānaṃ akusalānaṃ dhammānaṃ anuppādāya* .... *Uppannānaṃ pāpakānaṃ akusalānaṃ dhammānaṃ pahānāya* .... *Anuppannānaṃ kusalānaṃ dhammānaṃ uppādāya* ... *Uppannānaṃ kusalānaṃ dhammānaṃ ṭhitiyā asammosāya bhiyyo-bhāvāya vepullāya bhāvanāya pāripūriyā* ....

[3] *Dīgha*, Vol. III, p. 271.

CHAPTER VI

JHĀNA

(*Meditation*)

"In the words *jhāna*, contemplation, and *samādhi*, rapt concentration", says Mrs. Rhys Davids [1], "are contained the expression of that self-training in selective, intensive work of mind in which the Indian sought, by changing the usual conditions and procedure in cognition, to induce consciousness of a higher or different power". *Jhāna* or ecstatic musing was a very longstanding practice similar to the Yoga of the Hindus and the four *jhānas* consist in the process of systematic elimination of factors in consciousness.

Buddhaghosa, evidently following the authority of the *Dhammasaṅgaṇī*, speaks of five *jhānas*, a somewhat later classification which had developed out of the four *jhānas* described and differentiated in the Sutta portion of the Pāli canon. The four or five *jhānas* constitute a category by themselves and in many of the *Suttas* they are relegated to the *rūpāvacara* sphere of consciousness. In the *Abhidhammattha-Saṅgaha*, the five *jhānas* are mentioned as equally holding good in the case of the *lokuttara* state of consciousness. It is not, however, clearly stated anywhere in this authoritative Buddhist Manual why they should not also hold good in the case of the *kāmāvacara* or the *arūpāvacara* sphere. The discrimination made in favour of two out of the four *avacaras* would seem to have been an arbitrary procedure of thought. The four or five *jhānas*, considered apart from the four *avacaras*, signify nothing else than four or five stages in a process of *jhāna* from its inception to its termination in the attainment of a state of trance (*samāpatti*). Altogether five factors are involved in each process of *jhāna* at its inception, namely, *vitakka*, *vicāra*, *pīti*, *sukha* and *ekaggatā*. The first factor, *vitakka*, is rendered 'initial application' as it directs "its concomitant properties towards the object." *Vicāra* is rendered 'sustained application'

---

[1] *Buddhist Psychology*, 2nd Ed. pp. 94—95.

because it "permits the continued exercise of the thought on the object". *Pīti* is that factor in consciousness which creates an interest in the same object. *Sukha*, the fourth factor, is nothing but pleasurable, easeful and happy feeling which results from the attainment of the condition sought for, and *ekagattā* is the element of individualisation which develops from time to time into *samādhi*. Thus *ekaggatā* remains a common factor throughout the *jhānic* process. It is indeed the most essential condition of the entire process of *jhāna*. The so-called four or five *jhānas* signify no more than the four or five successive stages of the *jhānic* thought.

In the first stage of meditation five elements, viz., *vitakka*[1] *vicāra*, *pīti*[2], *sukha* and *ekaggatā* are present. In the second stage, the first two are eliminated. In the third, the first three are eliminated, leaving *sukha* and *ekaggatā*. In the fourth, *sukha* is replaced by *upekkhā* and there remain two elements, viz., *upekkhā* and *ekaggatā*. There is not much difference between these two sets of meditation. In the second stage of the first set of meditations, *vitakka* and *vicāra* disappear simultaneously, but in the second set of meditations, they disappear one after another, thus giving opportunity for another stage. The third, fourth and fifth stages of the second set of meditations correspond to the second, third and fourth stages of the first set.

As regards right concentration (*sammā-samādhi*), Buddhaghosa describes it as concentration on good thought. It is so called because in *samādhi*, all thoughts are simultaneously and rightly centred on a particular subject. Its characteristic is absence of distraction, its immediate cause is firmness and its remote cause is happiness. *Samādhi* has been variously divided according to its predominant characteristics. Regarding the purity and impurity of *samādhi*, Buddhaghosa points out that the condition which leads to its excellence, causes its purity, while that which causes deterioration,

---

[1] *Vitakka* is the directing of concomitant properties towards an object and *vicāra* is the continued exercise of the mind on that object and as regards *ekaggatā*, the mental property by which the object of consciousness, is necessarily regarded as an individual occupying a definite position in space or time or in both, and is termed an individuality of an object. *Vide*, Shwe Zan Aung's *Compendium of Philosophy*, pp. 56 foll.

[2] Signifies an interest in an object.

brings about its impurity. Buddhaghosa says that there are two ways of practising *samādhi*, viz., *lokiya* and *lokuttara*. The practice of *lokuttara samādhi* is but the culture of wisdom, while the practice of *lokiya samādhi* consists in purifying one's own conduct, establishing oneself in the purified conduct, destroying the ten obstacles, adopting the practice of one of the forty *kammaṭṭhānas*, avoiding living in a manner unsuitable to the practice of meditation, destroying the minor impediments and applying oneself to the perfect practice of meditation. It really means concentrative meditation. It is of an intensive attention, i.e., of concentration, establishing of consciousness exclusively and voluntarily on any single object [1].

It would seem that Buddhaghosa takes *samādhi* almost in the same sense as *jhāna*, in contravention of the usual sense in which the term *samādhi* is employed and understood in Indian literature. We have suggested above that *samādhi* or *samāpatti* marks the close of a period in the continued process of *jhāna*. The states of *samādhi* or trance are to be conceived as so many halting stations on the road. At each of these states, there is a dead stop, so to speak, of the thought-process in *jhāna*. The state is reached by two stages, namely, *upacāra* or access, and *appanā* or consummation. A new period begins when another *ārammaṇa* or object engages the attention and mind is concentrated thereon. After having gone through five stages, there occurs another state of trance and so on. The Pāli texts usually speak of nine *samāpattis* or states of *samādhi*, the first eight of which are said to have been reached or experienced by the Indian teachers already before the advent of the Buddha, while the ninth state called *saññāvedayitanirodha* was reached for the first time by the Buddha himself [2]. The period extending from the eighth to the ninth is broadly subdivided into eight stages or eight degrees of *lokuttara jhāna*. As expressly mentioned in the *Abhidhammatthasaṅgaha*, the thought-process in *jhāna* proceeds in the same manner as in the earlier stages. According to Buddhist treatment of the subject, the *Kāmāvacara* represents the non-*jhānic* or non-reflective sphere of thought. It denotes a level of consciousness when the subject is in touch with external objects as cognised

---

[1] *Majjhima*, III, pp. 71—78.

[2] *Majjhima Nikāya*, Vol. I, p. 296.

through the senses, the objects themselves being regarded as things belonging to an external order governed by its own *dhamma* (law of happening). In other words, the nine *samāpattis* are attainable in three higher spheres of thought and three higher levels of consciousness, namely, the *rūpāvacara*, the *arūpāvacara* and the *lokuttara*, the first four in the *rūpāvacara*, the next four in the *arūpāvacara* and the last in the *lokuttara*. These spheres of thought and levels of consciousness also constitute so many successive planes of direct experience. Thus the intensification of the degrees of concentration of mind is determined by the nature of the *ārammaṇa* or object. The further the mind travels away from the objects of sense, the percepts and images, the deeper is the concentration. The *jhāna*, thus considered, is to be viewed as a passage of thought from object to object until a complete isolation from all objects, bodily or mental, is accomplished. The idea of isolation is expressed by such terms as *viveka* (aloofness) or *vivitta* (aloof). It is also a process of self-purification through a gradual elimination of all disturbing and distressing factors in consciousness. The nature of the ninth *samāpatti* called *saññāvedayitanirodha*, in which the feeling of *vimutti* or the realisation of *nibbāna* is possible, is hinted at in the *Cullavedalla Sutta* of the *Majjhima Nikāya* (Vol. I). In this *Sutta*, we are told, that the state of trance is reached by the cessation, first of *vacīsaṅkhāra* (vocal functions), next of *kāyasaṅkhāra* (vital functions) and lastly of *cittasaṅkhāra* (mental functions). And inversely when the normal state of the individual is restored, there begins first the mental function, next the vital function and lastly the vocal function. We are further told that when consciousness enters into this state of trance, the individual becomes outwardly as good as dead, *usmā* or warmth remaining as the only palpable indication that the person is alive. Certain visions dawn on consciousness as it passes from state to state, from level to level and from plane to plane. The true vision is that which arouses the prospect of the goal. Certain *iddhis* or supernormal faculties also develop in the same process, but one is to beware of them so that they may not stand in the way. Buddhaghosa in his *Visuddhimagga* (pp. 168—169) speaks of five *jhānas*. With regard to *jhānas*, five kinds of *vasī* or mastery are obtained: (1) the power of reflecting on the *jhānic* thought (*āvajjanavasī*), (2) the power of attainment (*samāpajjana-*

vasī), (3) the power of resolution (*adiṭṭhānavasī*), (4) the power of exertion (*vuṭṭhānavasī*) and (5) the power of concentration (*paccavekkhanavasī*). A bhikkhu who has avoided the five pleasures of the senses, is said to have passed the range of vision of the evil one, who divested of pleasures and wrong state of mind, abides in the first ecstacy, the second ecstacy, the fourth ecstacy, the plane of infinity of consciousness, the plane of naught, the plane of neither perception nor non-perception, and the plane where feeling and perception cease [1]. In the *Jhāna-saṁyutta* of the *Saṁyutta Nikāya* [2], the Buddha points out that there are four classes of people who practise *jhāna*, (1) one who practises meditation is skilled in concentration, but is not skilled in the attainment thereof; (2) one who practises meditation is skilled in the attainment of concentration itself; (3) one who practises meditation is neither skilled in concentration nor skilled in the attainment thereof; and (4) one who practises meditation is skilled both in concentration and the fruits thereof. Of the four, the last one is the best and most pre-eminent.

Here we have to consider also the subject of *Satipaṭṭhāna* which constitutes a grammar of *jhāna*. *Sammāsati* means right recollection. It also means wakefulness of mind, alertness, self-consciousness. It is mindfulness with regard to body [3], sensation, mind and phenomenon (*dhamma*). The *Satipaṭṭhāna Sutta* of the *Majjhima Nikāya* contains the Buddha's advice to the monks to practise mindfulness. It is by the fourfold mastering of mindfulness that one can pass beyond sorrow and lamentation and ills of body and mind and obtain the right path [4].

---

[1] Cf. *Nivāpa Sutta*, *Majjhima Nikāya*, I, pp. 151—160.

[2] *Saṁyutta Nikāya*, III, p. 263—279.

[3] *Kāyagatāsati Sutta* (*Majjhima Nikāya*, III, pp. 88—89).

[4] *Majjhima Nikāya*, I, pp. 55—63; Cf. *Cakkavattisīhanādasuttanta*, *Dīgha*, III, pp. 58—79; *Aṅguttara Nikāya*, *Aṭṭhaka nipāta*, Vol. IV, pp. 150 foll.

CHAPTER VII

PUGGALA

(*Individuality and Personality*)

Puggala, *attā*, *satta* and *jīva* are the four terms which occur in the Buddhist texts in connection with all discussions relating to individual, individuality, personality, self and soul [1]. As a biological term, *puggala* is nowhere used to deny the existence of an individual being or a living person. When it is said, e.g., in the *Dhammapada* that the self is the lord of the self (*attā hi attano nātho*) [2] or in the *Mahāparinibbāna Suttanta*, "Be yourself your own lamp and your own refuge" (*atta-dīpā viharatha atta-saraṇā*) [3], by the word *atta* or 'self' is meant the living individual to whom the advice is given. Here the particular individual or individuals are beings that exist in fact, grow in time and ultimately die. Certain philosophical enquiries arise in connection with these individuals, the 'living souls' (to use an English phraseology). The question arises: how are the individuals known to us? How can they be represented in knowledge? And how far can the ultimate reality be realized in thought or experience?

These points are popularly discussed in the *Milindapañha*, in the very opening discussion. We are told that the individuals are signified by some names arbitrarily fixed, Nāgasena, Sūrasena or Vīrasena. The personal name is only a conventional device to denote an individual and to distinguish him from other individuals. It has no connotation beyond this symbolism. The name in itself is insufficient as a means of forming a complete idea of the individual concerned; when we proceed to represent the individual in knowledge, we only lay hold of certain percepts or concepts denoting the various aspects or factors. But the individual concerned is not

---

1 *Kathāvatthu*, I, p. 26.

2 *Verse* 160.

3 *Dīgha*, II, p. 100.

involved in the representation itself. The feeling, however, is that the percepts or concepts with which the representation is concerned, cannot be formed without some sort of reference to an individual and the reference is a whole reference, not mechanically divisible into parts. There never arises a position in thought where the equation of the whole with the sum total of parts is justified, nor can at the same time the notion of the whole be possible apart from the parts.

The point at issue is illustrated by the simile of a chariot and its parts. Chariot is a name or designation in common use by which a whole thing in its organic unity and working order is meant. But when one tries to lay hold on it, one lays one's finger only on parts. Even by mechanically summing up the parts, the idea of the whole which is sought to be conveyed, cannot be produced. The ideas of the parts arise with reference to an object which is not actually involved in them. The object of reference is not a permanent thing, while the concepts that are formed in thought with reference to it remain as abstract materials of thought (*vijjamāna paññattis*) [1]. As to a living human being, who too is not a permanent object in nature or in experience, the concepts or general ideas that may be formed in thought with reference to him are the five aggregates, *rūpa, vedanā, saññā* and the rest. The individuals come and go but the concepts as concepts remain as permanent materials of thought and as the possible modes of representation in thought or means of description in words. These are *vijjamāna paññattis* or concepts as abstract materials of thought.

This elucidation of the Buddhist view of *Puggala* in the *Milinda* is but an elaboration of the teaching of a *gāthā* ascribed in the *Saṃyutta Nikāya* to *Bhikkhunī* Vajirā [2]. The discussion in the *Milinda* presupposes an earlier controversy on this subject (*Puggalakathā*) in the *Kathāvatthu*, a book of controversies, which tradition entertains as a compilation of Asokan age. The controversy starts on the question of validity of a certain proposition (*paṭiññā*) which is to be regarded as a correct verbal representation of the view point or doctrine (*laddhi*) of a certain Buddhist school of thinkers called

---

[1] *Puggala Paññatti Commy*, P.T.S., pp. 171 foll.

[2] *Yathā hi aṅgasambhārā hoti*, etc., Vol. I (*Bhikkhunīvagga*).

Puggalavādins in Buddhaghosa's commentary. As Dr. Barua points out, there is a good deal of misrepresentation of the opponent's view point, the main intention of the orthodox defender of the good faith being only to establish a verbal interpretation of a verbal proposition with a view to taking a dialectical advantage over it [1]. There is an attempt throughout to show that the Puggalavādin's position is not different from that of outsiders who are avowedly the upholders of the doctrine of soul as a permanent entity. But reading between the lines, it is easy to make out clearly that where-ever the suggestion is made that the import of the point under discussion is identical with the view point of the outsiders, it is at once repudiated. The controversy is important as bringing out the exact Buddhist position with regard to the problem of *Puggala* or Individuality. The position upheld, on the whole, by the unknown Buddhist opponent may be reduced to this, that to talk about the five aggregates as *Vijjamāna paññattis* is to return no answer to the problem of individuality. If five aggregates be real as concepts or means of representation, they convey no meaning without reference to individuals in existence. Without such a reference the aggregates, posited as reals, are mere abstractions.

The problem of individuality is bound up with the problem of the ego, percipient or internal knower (*vedagū*). The problem of the ego has been discussed in the *Milinda*. The position of those who uphold the doctrine of the ego is stated thus: that there is an internal knower in every living self or individual who is the real seer of all things seen, the hearer of all things heard and so on (*vedagū upalabbhati*) [2]. The organs of sense stand as so many avenues through which the ego gathers experience of the external world. According to the Buddhist view as set forth in the *Milinda*, the ego thus conceived, does not satisfactorily account for the mental phenomena. If the tongue, the organ of taste, had not its local independence, the sweetness or bitterness of a thing could also have been tasted and discriminated even when the thing swallowed passes beyond the range of the tongue. The same holds true also in the case of other organs of sense. A scientific explanation of all

---

[1] *Prolegomena to a History of Buddhist Philosophy*, p. 34.

[2] *Milindapañho*, Trenckner, p. 54.

mental phenomena does not lie in a single cause such as the ego but in a conjuncture of causal circumstances (*paccaya-sāmaggi*). It is true, no doubt, that whenever any mental operation takes place, it takes place as a unit with regard to time, depending on the same subjective basis and stimulated by the same object (*ekavatthukā ekārammaṇā*)[1]. The Buddhist formula is: there must be the eye, the organ of sight, there must be a visible matter (*rūpa*), present within the range of vision (*āpāthagata*) and there must be auditory cognition, the combination of the three making the sense-impact (*phassa*) possible; this impact is a condition precedent of sensation. In searching for the ego which is believed to be the *sāra* or substratum of individuality, we tumble only upon certain sensations or perceptions or cognitions or volitions or predispositions but never the substratum itself. The usual description of ego is that it is permanent, invariable, eternal, firmly established like a wooden pillar of a city-gate and the same for ever (*Nicco dhuvo sassato esikaṭṭhāyiṭṭhito, sassati samaṃ ṭhassati*)[2]. But one will always appeal in vain to experience to furnish apodeictic certainty for the existence of such an entity as within the living self. The Buddhist psychologist introduces mind as an internal sense or *sensus communis* (*manindriya*), but he is far from positing it as an ego. But he admits the possibility of a state of consciousness when it has been free from all obsessions of objects. In this state consciousness can in no way be characterised (*ananuvejjo*)[3]. What happens to this consciousness after the death of the individual is not at all clear. But the Buddhist freely entertains the popular belief in rebirth. How can the process of rebirth be explained without the reality of the ego or soul is the question. This too has been discussed in the *Milinda*, as also in the *Kathāvatthu*. It goes without saying that the Buddhist thinker repudiates the notion of the passing of the ego from an embodiment to an embodiment. His is not a theory of transmigration of soul. The course of transmigration has been described in the *Bṛhat-Āraṇyaka Upaniṣad* by the simile of a grass-leech (*tṛṇajalaukā*) which passes from the end of one blade of grass to that of another. The *Bhelasaṃhitā* has sought to

[1] *Dhammapada commentary*, Vol. I, pt. I, p. 22.

[2] *Dīgha*, I, p. 14. *M.N.* I, p. 136.

[3] *M.N.*, I, 140.

show that the analogy is untenable (*na yuktaṃ*). With the Buddhist, rebirth is to be conceived as *kammasantati* or the continuity of an impulse. The point is illustrated by the instance of a set of lamps, each with fitness for ignition and placed in a row and in close touch with each other, one of which being lighted, the others are lighted. Here there is no passing of any spirit from one lamp to another. The lamp which is first lighted serves only to help in producing the necessary condition for ignition in the remaining lamps.

CHAPTER VIII

PAṬICCA-SAMUPPĀDA

(*Dependent Origination*)

Paṭiccasamuppāda is claimed to be the fundamental concept of Buddhism as a system of thought. The term has been variously interpreted both by the Buddhist scholiasts themselves and modern scholars without sufficiently bringing out its philosophical import and implications. They have sought to explain it either as a doctrine of causation or that of dependent origination or that of becoming by the way of a cause, by the usual and oft-recurring formula of twelve *Nidānas*. There are traditional expositions of the twelve *Nidānas* in many of the canonical texts and later commentaries both in Pāli and Sanskrit. There are several inscriptions referring to *Paṭiccasamuppāda* as the fundamental doctrine of Buddhism. It is difficult to realise the metaphysical significance of this doctrine. It behoves us, therefore, to see if the discussion of the problem of *Paṭiccasamuppāda* can be introduced in a new way.

The formula of twelve *Nidānas* must be taken to be a later appendage to an earlier formulation of the doctrine. The formula came in only by way of an illustration of the original formulation, which has been clearly set forth in the three Bodhi *suttas* in the *Udāna*. Similar formulations are also met with in some of the suttas of the *Majjhima Nikāya* [1]. There is at least one *sutta* [2] in the *Majjhima Nikāya* in which the original formulation is presented without the illustrative formula of twelve *Nidānas*. The Bodhi suttas in the *Udāna* clearly indicate three successive stages in the formulation of the doctrine: (1) *anuloma* or order of becoming, (2) *paṭiloma* or order of cessation (*nirodha*), (3) *anuloma-paṭiloma* being a synthesis of the order of becoming and the order of cessation. There were certain Buddhist schools, including the *Sarvāstivādins* in whose opinion the *anuloma* order only is valid. It is, therefore, not sur-

[1] *Majjhima Nikāya*, I, pp. 262 foll.

[2] *Cūḷasakuladāyi sutta*, *Majjhima Nikāya*, II, p. 32.

prising at all that in the texts only the *anuloma* order is recognised and explained. We cannot agree with Dr. P. C. Bagchi that the non-recognition of the *paṭiloma* order on the part of the *Sarvāstivādins* disproves the earlier date of formulation of the doctrine in the *paṭiloma* order as well [1]. Buddhaghosa was well aware of this viewpoint and he has sought to repudiate it in his *Visuddhimagga* [2]. Buddhaghosa says that according to some "the doctrine of *Paṭiccasamuppāda* deals with the problem of becoming (*uppāda*) only". That is not proper. Why? (1) Because there is no text to support it; (2) because it militates against what is stated in the *suttas*; (3) because it cannot be deduced from a grammatical construction of the term itself [3]. All that the Pāli scholiast seeks to establish is that the statement of the doctrine is not complete, if the aspect of *nirodha* is precluded, and that throughout the Pāli texts we meet with both the aspects of the doctrine.

The doctrine of *Paṭiccasamuppāda* has been introduced in some of the typical *suttas* as *majjha* or the way of the golden mean. It is by this *majjha* that the founder of the system is said to have established his position avoiding the two extremes of *atthi* and *natthi* [4], theism and atheism, eternalism and annihilationism, fatalism or determinism [5] and the theory of chance [6] or fortuitous origination, and of moral freedom [7] and bondage.

The doctrine of *Paṭiccasamuppāda* in its simplest formulation runs as follows: — *Imasmiṃ sati idaṃ hoti; imass' uppādā idaṃ upapajjati; imasmiṃ asati idaṃ na hoti; imassa nirodhā idaṃ nirujjhatīti* [8].

[1] *E.I.* Vol. XI, pp. 194 ff & 199 ff.

[2] Vol. II, p. 518: *Keci pana uppādamattaṃ paṭiccasamuppādo ti vadanti. Taṃ na yujjati.*

[3] *Visuddhimagga*, II, pp. 518—519: *Keci pana paṭiccasammā ca titthiyaparikappita-pakatipurisādikāraṇa-nirapekkho uppādo paṭiccasamuppādo ti evaṃ uppādamattaṃ paṭiccasamuppādo ti vadanti. Taṃ na yujjati. Kasmā?* (1) *Suttābhāvato,* (2) *suttavirodhato,* (3) *gambhīranayāsambhavato,* (4) *saddabhedato ca.*

[4] *Saṃyutta. N.* II, pp. 77 & 96; *S. N.*, III, p. 1,5.

[5] *Sabbam pubbe katahetu, A. N.*, I, p. 173.

[6] *Sabbam ahetu-appaccayā, adhiccasamuppannā, A.N.*, III, p. 440.

[7] *Sukhadukkhaṃ sayaṃkataṃ sukhadukkham paraṃkatam, Peṭakopadesa*, Ch. I; *Pre-Buddhistic Indian Philisophy*, pp. 406—407.

[8] *Majjhima Nikāya*, II, p. 32.

"This having been, that comes to be; from the arising of this that arises. This having not been, that does not come to be; from the cessation of this, that ceases to be". This in illustrated by the oft-recurring formula of twelve *Nidānas*. The Buddhist scholiasts have sought to explain the earlier form so as to make it fit in with the formula of twelve *Nidānas*. But the question remains — What is the correct interpretation of the *Paṭiccasamuppāda* as stated in the above form, apart from any reference to the formula of twelve *Nidānas*? Does it imply a mere order of sequence of facts as experienced and noted, or a fully developed doctrine of causation? So far as we can make out, it is rather a natural basis of the doctrine of causation than the doctrine of causation itself. The sequence is nothing but an order in which snapshots of things are taken and noted down, with the result that the facts as registered, come as disconnected data of experience. In introducing a logical interconnection between these facts, we have recourse to a law of causation. The idea of sequence implies an antecedent (*purejāta*) and a consequent (*pacchājāta*). Explained in the light of causation, the antecedent is not a single cause but a combination of certain circumstances with causal efficiency to account for the occurrence of the consequent. The causal circumstances, when analysed and classified and differentiated, yield the conception of a number of *paccayas* or rational modes of representing the nature of *dhammatā* in thought. As for sequence as expressing the nature of reality as commonly experienced, it is not something which mind imagines but something which forces itself on mind. This led some of the Buddhist schools to speak of *Paṭiccasamuppāda* as *asaṅkhatadhātu* or uncreated element [1]. The textual authority cited in support of this view is as follows: — "Whether, monks, there be an arising of *Tathāgatas*, or whether there be no such arising, in each this nature of things just stands, this causal status, this causal orderliness, the relatedness of this to that. Concerning that the *Tathāgata* is fully enlightened, that he fully understands. Fully enlightened, fully understanding, he declares it, teaches it, reveals it, sets it forth, manifests, explains, makes it plain saying: 'Behold! conditioned by this, that comes to be" [2].

[1] *Kathāvatthu*, Vol. II, p. 319.

[2] *The Book of the Kindred Sayings*, Vol. II, p. 21.

The *Abhidhammattha-saṅgaha* rightly points out that the *Paṭicca-samuppāda* mode (*naya*) differs from the *Paṭṭhāna* mode in this respect that it is just concerned with sequence in the procession of events or phenomena as observed (*tabbhāva tabbhāvī*) while the *Paṭṭhāna* mode is concerned with the differentiation of the various *paccayas* or causal factors involved in the causal relation. The difference in view may perhaps be better expressed if we say that the *Paṭiccasamuppāda* mode is concerned with a dynamic view of the *Paṭṭhāna* mode with a static view of nature or reality. Turning to the oft-recurring formula of twelve *Nidānas* we find that *avijjā* is generally allowed to head the list. The term is generally rendered as ignorance, which does not, however, bring out the philosophical connotation of the term. As regards *avijjā*, Buddhaghosa has raised and discussed a very interesting point. Can *avijjā* as conceived in Buddhism be treated as an uncaused root-principle like the *mūla-prakṛti* of the Sāṅkhya philosophy? The Pāli scholiast maintains, no doubt in agreement with some of the earlier exponents of Buddhism, that *avijjā* is not conceived on the lines of Sāṅkhya *mūlaprakṛti*. With the Buddhists, *avijjā* is not uncaused: Buddhaghosa has however to admit that there are some texts in which *avijjā* may appear to be similar to the *mūlaprakṛti* of the Sāṅkhya system. He refers in connection to a text in the *Aṅguttara Nikāya* in which the Buddha is represented as saying: "the beginning of *avijjā* does not appear so that one might say that ignorance did not exist formerly but it has since come into being. However it is apparent that *avijjā* is conditioned". "The beginning of *bhavataṇhā* does not appear so that one might say that *bhavataṇhā* did not exist formerly but it has since come to being. However it is apparent that *bhavataṇhā* is conditioned". Thus the Buddha sought to account for the cosmic process of the cycle of births and deaths by mentioning two specific conditions of actions.

The Pāli scholiasts ought to have considered along with it the other statement which occurs in the *Saṁyutta Nikāya* (*Anamata saṁyutta*). In the *Saṁyutta* text the Buddha is represented as saying: "Incalculable (endless) is the process of *saṃsāra*, the beginning of beings running through the course of *saṃsāra* being cloaked by *avijjā* and tied to *bhavataṇhā* does not appear" [1].

[1] *Saṃyutta Nikāya*, II, p. 186.

All this amounts to saying that endless is the cosmic process, the course of *saṃsāra*, so that its beginning ever remains unknown and unknowable. Thus the entire history of *saṃsāra* may never be unveiled. But the *dhammatā* of the process is definitely known. The *dhammatā* in question consists in the related character of reality in its process of becoming. If one knows this *dhammatā*, it is immaterial whether one has the historical knowledge of the entire course of *saṃsāra* or not. At whichever point one takes up its consideration, it involves two factors, namely, *avijjā* and *bhavataṇhā*, that are sufficient to account for the happy or unhappy states of beings. *Avijjā* is that factor which keeps the nature of *dhammatā* concealed, and *bhavataṇhā* is that factor which constitutes an incessant impulse to becoming. All forms of ignorance are expressions of *avijjā*, and all kinds of desires are various manifestations of *bhavataṇhā*. It is in this manner that Buddhism meets and answers agnosticism which draws a huge capital out of man's incapability to know the first beginning of the world.

It has been well pointed out by Rhys Davids that the doctrine of *Paṭiccasamuppāda* finds in the *Mahānidāna Suttanta* of the *Dīgha Nikāya* (Vol. II, pp. 55 foll), the fullest exposition accorded to it throughout the *Piṭakas*. The *Dīghabhāṇakas* or the reciters of long discourse excluded the first two of the 12 *nidānas* or chapters, viz., *avijjā* (ignorance) and *saṇkhāra* (confections). In the *Paccayākāravibhaṅga* of the *Abhidhamma Piṭaka*, the formula is reiterated and analysed with greater variety of presentation. But in the *Mahānidāna Suttanta* the doctrinal contents are more fully worked out. Although the formula as expounded in this *sutta* ends in the usual way — such is the uprising of the whole body of ill, — the burden of the dialogue is in no way directly concerned with ill, pain or sorrow. In certain other passages where the *nidāna* chain occurs, *dukkha* occupies the foreground (*Dialogues of the Buddha*, II, p. 42). *Saṇkhāra* is Sanskrit *Saṃskāra*, which means an aggregation. *Avijjā* (ignorance) is the cause of aggregation. *Taṇhā* is also interpreted as thirst, craving. According to the *Cūḷataṇhā-saṅkhaya Sutta* [1] a bhikkhu wins deliverance by the extirpation of cravings so as to become consummate in perfection in his union with peace and in the higher life and foremost among gods and men. Sensation

[1] *Majjhima Nikāya*, 1, 151 foll.

is the cause of thirst. *Vedanā* means sensation or feeling which is pleasurable or painful. *Saḷāyatana* is the six organs and objects of sense, viz., *Rūpa*, *Vedanā*, *Saññā*, *Saṅkhāra* and *Viññāṇa*.

Viññāṇa is consciousness which, according to the Buddha, runs on and continues without break of identity [1]. All sinful acts may be traced to *avijjā* or ignorance. All wrong states have their origin in ignorance [2]. It is clear that from contact arises feeling [3].

According to the Buddha, the only ideal worth striving after, is the ideal of a perfect life in this present existence, in saintship and this ideal is to be reached by freedom from desire [4].

In the *Nidāna Saṃyutta* of the *Saṃyutta Nikāya* [5] we find that the Buddha explained to the bhikkhus the chain of causation which begins with ignorance and ends with birth, old age and death leading to grief, lamentation, suffering, sorrow, and despair. In the chain of causation, we find that six senses originate from name and form. In the *Saḷāyatana saṃyutta* of the *Saṃyutta Nikāya* [6] the Blessed One speaks of the six senses. He points out that the eye and the objects of sight, the ear and the sounds, the nose and the sense, the tongue and the savours, the body and the things tangible, the mind and the mind's state are all impermanent, ill, and void of the self. But there is the way of escape from these. This is the restraint of desire and lust which are in the eye, etc. Where there is no desire, there is no ill. He further points out that by seeing the six senses as impermanent, as fetters and as *āsavas*, ignorance is removed and knowledge arises; fetters are abandoned and *āsavas* (sins) are uprooted. The Buddha characterises the eye and the object of sight, the ear and the sounds, etc., as transitory. According to him passion is a disease and one can abide passionless by not imagining "I have an eye", etc. One should not be enamoured of the object cognisable by the eye, etc. If one is so, then one is called restrained. If one is not so, then one is said to have lack of restraint [7]. We find that from *phassa* or contact *vedanā* or feeling

[1] Cf. *Mahātaṇhāsaṅkhaya sutta*, *M. N.* I, 256 foll.
[2] Cf. *Opamma Saṃyutta*, *S.N.* II. pp. 262—272.
[3] Cf. *Dhātu-Saṃyutta*, *S.N.* II, pp. 140 foll.
[4] *Udāna*, chapter I.
[5] Pt. II, pp. 1—33.
[6] Vol. IV, pp. 201—204.
[7] Cf. *Saḷāyatana-Saṃyutta*, *S.N.* Vol. IV, pp. 1—204.

arises. In the *Vedanā saṃyutta* of the *Saṃyutta Nikāya* [1], we find that there are three *vedanās* or feelings: — Feeling that is pleasant, feeling that is painful, and feeling that is neither pleasant nor painful. The lurking tendency, to lust for pleasant feeling, to repugnance for painful feeling and to ignorance of feeling that is neither pleasant nor painful, must be abandoned. Pleasant feeling should be regarded as an ill, painful feeling as a barb and neutral feeling as impermanent. So all these should be abandoned. This abandonment in a bhikkhu is called rightly seeing [2].

In the *Paccayākāra-Vibhaṅga,* various *paccayas* are enumerated and explained, after which the *suttanta* portion naturally closes. According to this *Vibhaṅga, avijjā* or ignorance means ignorance in suffering, in the origin of suffering, in the cessation of suffering and in the path leading to the cessation of suffering.

As regards confections or conformations, we find conformations of merit, demerit, body, mind and speech. There is good thought in the domain of sensual pleasure and in the domain of form, conducive to charity and virtue. The reverse of it is found in *apuññābhisaṃkhāra,* confections regarding demerit. As regards consciousness, it is consciousness as regards sight, hearing, scent, tongue, body and mind. There is name and there is form. The name consists of *vedanā* (feeling), *saññā* (perception) and *saṃkhāra* (confection). The form consists of the element of four great beings.

As regards contact, it is contact with regard to eye, ear, nose, tongue, body and mind. There is sensation due to sight, due to hearing, due to smelling, due to taste, due to bodily action and thought. There is desire for form, sound, scent, taste, touch, and *dhamma* or thing. There is attachment for sensual pleasure, false notion, etc. *Bhava* or existence is of two kinds: — existence as a state of action and existence as a state of origination. As regards the existence as a state of action, we may speak of the confection of merit and demerit, etc., and as regards the existence as a state or origination, we may speak of the coming into being, form, formlessness, etc. Then as regards birth, it means the existence of beings and the origination of *Khandhas* or the constituent elements. Then as regards old age and death, there is infirmity of beings and the

[1] IV, 204—238.

[2] Cf. *Vedanāsaṃyutta, S.N.,* IV, 204—238.

ripeness of *indriyas* or senses. Regarding death, it is nothing but disappearance of the human beings and the destruction of *khandhas* and life-senses.

Name and Form originate from consciousness and from Name originates ignorance. From sensation, desire, contact, attachment and ignorance originate. Name is nothing but an aggregate of sensation, perception and confection. Six senses originate from name and form, viz., eye, ear, nose, tongue, body and mind.

CHAPTER IX

KAMMAVĀDA

(*Doctrine of Kamma*)

The Pāli term denoting the doctrine of *Karma* is *Kammavāda* the alternative form of which is *Kiriyāvāda* [1]. The doctrine of *Karma* is accepted in all the main systems of Indian philosophy and religion as an article of faith. The Buddha is generally credited with the propounding of this doctrine but there is a clear statement in the *Majjhima Nikāya* to show that the doctrine had not originated with the Buddha. The statement is to the effect that the doctrine was propounded before the advent of the Buddha by an Indian teacher who was a householder [2].

According to the popular Hindu belief, *Karma* is a sum total of man's action in a previous birth, determining his future destiny which is unalterable. Its effect remains until it is exhausted through suffering or enjoyment. This popular notion of *Karma* is exemplified by a birth-story called *Matakabhatta Jātaka*.

The two extreme views of thought having a bearing upon the doctrine of *Karma* are stated thus in Buddhism: (1) sabbam *pubbe katahetu*, all that a being suffers from or experiences is due to the sum total of his deeds in the past; (2) *sabbaṃ ahetu appaccayā*, all that a being experiences in this life is only a matter of chance.

These two extremes are sought to be avoided in Buddhism. Jainism, which too claims to be a rightly formulated doctrine of action (*Kiriyā*) as distinguished from fatalism or determinism on the one hand, and the doctrine of chance on the other, takes up a position which is not acceptable to the Buddhists. Partly determined and partly not determined (*niyatāniyata*), or 'partly due to external causes and partly due to oneself' is taken to be the declared position of Jainism, which has been severely criticised in the *Devadaha sutta* [3].

---

[1] *Majjhima Nikāya*, I, p. 483.

[2] *Ibid.*, p. 483.

[3] *Ibid*, Vol. II, pp. 214 foll.

Let us see if the Buddhist statement crediting an earlier Indian teacher with the propounding of the doctrine of *Karma* is correct. In the *Bṛhat Āraṇyaka Upaniṣad* and in the teachings of Yājñavalkya we meet with a clear formulation of the doctrine of *Karma*, and the resemblance between this formulation and that which is met with in the Pāli texts, is so close that one may be perfectly justified in maintaining that the Buddhist doctrine of *Karma* is nothing but a further elucidation of that in the *Upaniṣad*. The *Kammavibhaṅga suttas* in the *Majjhima Nikāya* [1] are nothing but a later exposition of this doctrine. A still later exposition is found in the *Atthasālinī* of Buddhaghosa [2]. The doctrine is emphatically formulated in the *Cūḷakammavibhaṅga sutta* [3] in the following words: "*Kammassakā sattā kammadāyādā kammayonī kammabandhū kammapaṭisaraṇā. Kammaṃ satte vibhajati yadidaṃ hīṇappaṇītatāyāti.*" *Karma* is one's own, a man is an inheritor of his *karma*, one finds one's birth according to his or her *karma*, *karma* is one's own kith and *karma* is one's own refuge, *karma* divides beings into higher or lower.

Thus it may be shown that the earlier trends of thought were recognised and explained also in Buddhism but the question arises if such was precisely the Buddhist conception of *Karma*. It is indicated in many of the texts that violence should not be done to the accepted beliefs of the people, if these are found to be beneficial to their moral development. But the Buddhists approached the problem from a purely mental point of view. The Buddhist viewpoint has been characteristically set forth in the *Mahāniddesa* under *Jarā sutta*. The *Mahāniddesa* points out [4] that a man need not be afraid of the vast accumulation of *Karma* through a long cycle of births and rebirths. For considered from the point of view of mind the whole of such accumulation may be completely undone by a momentary action of mind. Mind is in its own place and as such can make and unmake all such accumulations of *Karma*.

[1] *Majjhima Nikāya*, III.

[2] pp. 63 foll.

[3] *Majjhima Nikāya*, III, p. 203.

[4] Vol. I, pp. 117—118:

Jīvitaṃ attabhāvo ca sukhadukkhā ca kevalā ekacittasamāyuttā, lahuso vattati-kkhaṇo.

Anidhānagatā bhaṅgā, puñjo n'atthi anāgate, nibbattā yeva tiṭṭhanti āragge sāsapūpamā.

On the whole Buddhism shifted the emphasis to the action and state of the mind. Accordingly *Karma* came to be defined as *Cetanā* or volition. A person can not be held morally or legally responsible for any action of his or her, if it is not intentional. Thus the Buddhist teachers tried to define *Karma* on a rational and practical basis. This point of view has, however, been shortly criticised by the *Sūtrakritāṅga* [1]. In the system of the *Abhidhamma* the Buddhist teachers seek to furnish the psychological data of ethics, men's conduct or external behaviour being regarded as an outward expression of his internal character. The accepted Buddhist idea of the doctrine of *Karma* may be represented by Buddhaghosa's expositions.

Buddhaghosa in his *Atthasālinī* [2] defines *Karma* as volition expressed in action (*Cetanāhaṃ bhikkhave kammam vadāmi*). An action is no action until the will is manifested in conduct. *Kamma* means consciousness of good and bad, merit and demerit (*Kammaṃ nāma kusalākusala-cetanā*) [3]. *Kamma* is of four kinds, (1) *Diṭṭhadhamma-vedaniya*, i.e., *Kamma* which produces result in this life, (2) *Upapaccavedaniya*, i.e., *kamma* which produces result in the next life, (3) *Aparāpariyāyavedaniya*, i.e., *karma* which produces result from time to time [4], and (4) *Ahosikamma*, i.e., past *kamma*. We have another fourfold division of *kamma*: — (1) *Garuka*, i.e., an act, be it good or bad, which has a serious result, (2) *Bahula*, i.e., excess of either virtue or vice which produces its respective results, (3) *Āsanna*, i.e., *karma* which is thought of at the time of death, and (4) *Kaṭattākamma*, i.e., an act which has been frequently done by one in his life-time, and which in the absence of the three previous *kammas*, causes rebirth. We have still another classification of *kamma*: (1) *Janaka*, (determining the character of rebirth), (2) *Upatthambhaka*, (sustaining), (3) *Upapiḷaka*, (oppressive) and (4) *Upaghātaka*, (hurting). These twelve kinds of acts and consequences are manifested in their true aspect in the Buddha's knowledge of the consequences of *karma*. Those who are endowed with the spiritual

---

[1] *Jaina sūtras*, Pt. II, S.B.E.

[2] pp. 88 foll.

[3] *Visuddhimagga*, II, p. 614.

[4] *Visuddhimagga*, II, p. 601.

insight come to know some *kammantara* and *vipākantara* [1]. *Kamma* produces consequence, retribution is born of action, action is the cause of rebirth, in this way the world continues. No action passes from the past life to the present, nor from the present to the future[2]. Regarding the relationship between *kamma* and *vipāka* Buddhaghosa says that there is no *kamma* in *vipāka*, and no *vipāka* in *kamma*. Each of them by itself is void, at the same time there is no *vipāka*. Just as there is no fire in the Sun, nor in the lense nor in the dried cow-dung and likewise fire is not outside them but comes into existence on account of their requisites, in the same way *vipāka* is not seen within the *kamma* nor outside it. A *kamma* is void of its *vipāka* which comes through *kamma*. *Vipāka* comes into existence on account of *kamma* [3]. In the past, the *khandhas*, which originated as the consequences of action (volition), ceased. In this existence other *khandhas* arise out of the consequences of past deeds. There is no condition which has come to this existence from the past, in this existence the *khandhas* which are originated on account of the consequences of *karma* are destroyed. In another existence others will be produced from this existence, not a single condition will pass on to the next existence [4]. According to the *Atthasālinī*, *Karma* is of three kinds: *Kāyakamma*, *Vacīkamma* and *Manokamma*. It is *Cetanā* and the states associated with it. According to Childers, all three originate in *cetanā*. He further points out that *karma* under the name of *saṃkhāra* is one of the links of *Paṭiccasamuppāda* [5]. Buddhaghosa divides *kamma* into (1) *Kammasamuṭṭhāna* (set up by *Karma*), (2) *Kammapaccaya* (caused by *Karma*), (3) *Kammapaccayacittasamuṭṭhāna* (caused by *Karma* and set up by consciousness), (4) *Kammapaccayaāhāra samuṭṭhāna* (caused by *Karma* and set up by sustenance), (5) *Kammapaccayautusamuṭṭhān* (caused by *Karma* and set up by temperature). *Kamma* is ultimately reduced to the psychological factor of volition. Volition is the unique determination of will. Will exercise has its power over its co-existent mental properties and

[1] *Visuddhimagga*, II. p. 602.
[2] *Visuddhimagga*, II, 603.
[3] *Visuddhimagga*, II. p. 603.
[4] *Visuddhimagga*, II. p. 603.
[5] p. 178.

physical qualities. In fact all our activities in deed, word or thought are due to its influence. The doctrine of *Karma* or the efficacy of good or bad works is inseparably bound up with that of renewed existence. The world exists through *karma* and people live through *karma* (*kammanā vattati loko, kammanā vattati pajā*).

CHAPTER X

DHAMMA

There is no other word or term in Buddhism, which is of so frequent occurrence as *dhamma* or its Sanskrit equivalent *dharma.* This term, precisely as in the Vedic texts, is used in both singular and plural forms. *Dhammatā* or *dharmatā* is coined by the Buddhists as a special term to signify the essential nature of things, the normal condition, the usual course [1]. In actual usage, however, the distinction in meaning between *dharma* and *dharmatā* is not strictly maintained. Mrs. Rhys Davids rightly points out that the word *dharma* has, in the history of Buddhist thought, undergone much elaboration, more so than in Brahmanic. Whether in its singular or plural form, it occurs only ten times in the Three Vedas; it is given no special consideration, historical or other, in a standard work like Oldenberg's *Religion des Veda* [2].

Childers suggests that the word, in masculine or neuter form, conveys such meaning in English as 'nature, condition, quality, property, characteristic, function, practice, duty, object, thing, idea, phenomenon, doctrine, law, virtue, piety, justice, the law or truth of Buddha, the Buddhist scriptures, and religion.' Similar is indeed the list of meanings suggested by Monier Williams in his Sanskrit-English Dictionary. The Pāli-English Dictionary, compiled by Rhys Davids and Stede, gives a more methodical treatment of the word classifying the various meanings in which it is employed in Buddhism. But even here the treatment fails of its purpose inasmuch as it does not set forth the reason why and how the word came to comprehend such a wide range of meaning without any fear of contradiction or inconsistency on the part of those who used it. The *Dhammapada-commentary* suggests that the word *dhamma* has been used in Pāli in one or other or all of these four meanings, (1)

---

[1] *Dīgha-Nikāya,* Vol. I I, pp. 12 ff. "*Dhammatā esā bhikkhave . . . . ayaṁ ettha dhammatā.*"

[2] *Buddhism,* revised edn., p. 82.

guṇa (quality, property, characteristic), (2) *desanā* (discourse, instruction), (3) *pariyatti* (worded doctrine of Buddha, scriptures), and (4) *nissatta-nijjīva-dhammā* (mental states, conditions or phenomena without involving the notion of ego or entity) [1]. The utmost that we here have, is no definition but a bare statement or cataloguing of four different meanings in which the word or term has been employed in early Buddhism.

Some guidance is given by Mrs. Rhys Davids [2] and Professor Stcherbatsky [3] in the matter of understanding and appreciating the Buddhist conception of *dhamma* or *dharma*.

The definitions of the term *dhamma* or *dharma* as met with in the Buddhist and Brahmanical works are all one-sided, not to say farfetched. We read, for instance, in the *Khuddakapāṭha-commentary* (p. 19):

'*Maggaphalanibbānāni dhammo' ti eke, 'bhāvitamaggānaṁ sacchikatanibbānānañ ca apāyesu apatanabhāvena dhāraṇato paramassāsavidhānato ca maggavirāgā eva imasmiṁ atthe dhammo' ti amhākaṁ khanti, Aggapasādanasuttañ c'ettha sādhakaṁ, vuttaṁ h'etaṁ: 'yāvatā bhikkhave dhammā saṁkhatā, ariyo aṭṭhaṅgiko maggo tesaṁ aggam akkhāyati.*'

"According to some authorities, *dhamma* means the efforting and fruition stages of the elect culminating in *nibbāna*. Our opinion, however, is that *dhamma* is that which 'up-holds' (*dhāraṇato*) in the sense that those who have cultivated the path and realised *nibbāna* have no longer the fear of fall into the states of woe, and no less in the sense that it provides for the highest kind of solace and ultimately transcends all need of effort. The teaching of the *Aggapasādanasutta* proves the truth of this. There it is said: As many doctrines, O Bhikkhus, have (so far) been formulated, the Noble Eightfold Path appears to be the best of them."

According to Jaimini's *Pūrvamīmāṃsāsūtra* (1. 1.2) *Codanālakṣaṇo'rtho dharmaḥ*.

"*Dharma* is that which is characterised by an urge into action fulfilling the (desired) object":

According to Manu's Code (Ed, Jolly, p. 14):

Vidvadbhiḥ sevitaḥ sadbhiḥ nityam adveṣarāgibhiḥ

---

[1] *Dhammapada-commentary*, Vol. I, p. 22.

[2] *Buddhism*, First and Revised Editions.

[3] *I.H.Q.*, Vol. X, No. 4, pp. 737 foll.

hṛdayenābhyanujñāto yo dharmas taṁ nibodhata.

"Comprehend that (alone) to be *dharma* which is cultivated by the learned, the elect, the persons who are always free from hatred and passion, and which is (at the same time) readily responded to by the heart."

According to the consensus of opinion, the Brahmanical definition of *dharma* is:

Vaidikaḥ pratipādyo'rthaḥ dharmaḥ
Vihitakriyayāsādhyo dharmaḥ puṁsāṁ guṇo mataḥ
Pratisiddhakriyāsādhyaḥ sa guṇo dharmaḥ ucyate.

"*Dharma* is an end to be attained in conformity with injunctions in the Vedas."

"*Dharma* is to be considered a distinctive quality of men to be achieved by means of action (work, conduct) as enjoined (in the Vedas)."

Referring to Asokan use of the word, Mrs. Rhys Davids opines: "The word *dhamma* is not 'morality' as it is unfortunately rendered in the *editio princeps*, nor is it 'law' or 'good form'. Senart's 'religion' is better, but too ambiguous. F. W. Thomas' definition 'based on revelation and custom' and 'a sphere of conduct leading to heaven' is a better guide. But why the weighty, the lofty term for 'that which ought to be done or not done,' namely 'conscience,' is never used by translators is strange. Or if not 'conscience' then at least, 'duty.' Externally considered, *dharma* is, for India, 'law'; for Buddhism, 'worded doctrine'. As belonging to man's inner world 'conscience' or 'duty' is more fit. It is the urge of this 'sense' that makes a man truly 'moral'. Because of that urge he (Aśoka) wards his fellowman in his person and in his interests." [1]

In Varuṇa the Vedic sages arrived at the conception of an ordered universe where everything happens according to Law and nothing by the caprice of an arbitrary will. And in *ṛta* they reached the conception of rhythmical evolution or harmonious manifestation of the cosmos. Both of these conceptions constituted the historical or philosophical background of the later ideas of *satya* and *dharma*. In the *Taittirīya Upaniṣad*, I. 1, *ṛta* and *satya* are introduced as two aspects of one and the same idea or reality — *pratyakṣa-Brahman*: *Pratyakṣam Brahmaṁ vadiṣyāmi, ṛtaṁ vadiṣyāmi, satyam vadiṣyāmi.*

[1] *Buddhism*, revised edn., p. 228.

In another passage of the same Upaniṣad, I. 9, *ṛta* and *satya* are mentioned along with *tapa*, *dama*, and the rest as different items of one and the same system of conduct or duty:

"*Ṛtaṁ ca svādhyāyapravacane ca Satyaṁ ca svādhyāyapravacane ca. Tapaś ca svādhyāyapravacane ca.*"

In a valedictory address in the same *Upaniṣad*, I. 11, we read:

"*Satyaṁ vada. Dharmaṁ cara. Svādhyāyān mā pramadaḥ. Satyān na pramaditavyaṁ. Dharmān na pramaditavyaṁ. Kusalān na pramaditavyaṃ.*"

"Speak the truth. Practise *dharma*. Do not neglect the study of the Vedas. A right-minded man must not deviate from truth, from *dharma*, and from good."

Thus in the third passage where the word *ṛta* does not occur, the word *dharma* is substituted for it; *dharma* takes the place of *ṛta*. What is the relation either between *ṛta* and *satya*, or between *satya* and *dharma*?

We might suggest that *satya* is that which is in conformity with *ṛta*, [1] and *ṛta* is that which is in conformity with *satya*, and the same as to the relation between *satya* and *dharma*. Or, we might say that *ṛta* assumes the name of *satya* when its nature is stated in terms of words, and that of *dharma* when its nature is manifested in the form of practice, duty or conduct. From one point of view, the whole programme of duty arises out of the primary idea of *ṛta*, and from another point of view, the whole programme of duty is comprehended by *dharma*. For the use of *dharma* in the sense of genus and species, whole and part, in the same breath, we may cite here the Pāli gāthā: [2]

Yass'ete caturo dhammā vānarinda yathā tava.
Saccaṁ dhammo dhitī cāgo diṭṭhaṁ so ativattati.

"He who is armed with these four *dharma* (principles), truth, piety, forbearance and self-sacrifice, overcomes the foe."

The relation between *satya* and *dharma* [3] as two aspects of one

---

[1] *Anṛta* which is an antithesis to *satya* is that which is not in conformity with *ṛta*.

[2] *Vānarinda Jātaka* (Fausboll, No. 57), Vol. I, p. 280.

[3] For the juxtaposition of the two words *satya* and *dharma*, or *dharma* and *satya*, *Cf. Chāndogya Upaniṣad*, VII, 2.1: *dharmaṁ cādharmaṁ ca, satyaṁ cānṛtaṁ ca sādhu cāsādhu ca hṛdyajñaṁ cāhṛdyajñaṁ ca.*

and the same idea or reality is emphatically brought out in the *Bṛhadāraṇyaka Upaniṣad*, I. 4. 14.

Satyaṁ vai tat. Tasmāt satyaṁ vadantaṁ āhur dharmaṃ vadatīti, dharmaṁ vā vadantaṁ satyaṁ vadatītyetaddhyevaitad ubhayaṁ bhavati.

"Dharma is indeed *satya*. Therefore they say that if a man declares *satya*, he declares *dharma*, and if he declares *dharma*, he declares *satya*. Thus both are the same."

In this text *dharma* stands for 'law,' 'principle of justice,' 'sphere of conduct' in conformity with established custom,' the disregard of, or departure from which is punishable by law. For here we also read:

Sa .... tacchreyorūpam atyasṛjata dharmaṁ. Tadetat kṣatrasya kṣatraṁ. Yad dharmas tasmād dharmāt paraṁ nāstyato abalīyāṁ balīyāṁ samāśamsate dharmena yathā rājñai.

"He created still further the most excellent Law (Dharma). Law is the *kṣatra* (power) of the *kṣatra*, therefore there is nothing higher than the Law. Thenceforth even a weak man rules a stronger with the help of the Law, as with the help of a king".

The meaning of the all-important dictum *dharmaḥ kṣatrasya kṣatraḥ* requires some amount of elaboration. Here *kṣatra* stands for both the earthly ruler and his divine prototype. When they say *dharma* is the *kṣatra* of the *kṣatra*, they mean that *dharma* is the guiding principle of royal administration, which is the same as to say the domination by the warrior-power has its justification or fulfilment only in the maintenance of the social order and the administration of justice. The king in his person is not above the law. It is the law that is above the king.

This conception of *dharma* was elaborated in early Buddhism. But with the Buddha, the Buddhist *dharma* is no mere law but something more than law; it is the principle of righteousness in conformity with which a reigning king is to shape his conduct and guide the course of administration.

Ko pana bhante rañño .... rājā ti? Dhammo bhikkhū ti Bhagavā avoca. Idha bhikkhave rājā cakkavattī dhammiko dhammarājā dhammaṁ yeva nissāya dhammaṁ sakkaronto dhammaṁ garukaronto dhammaṁ apacāyamāno dhammaddhajo dhammaketu dhammādhipateyyo dhammikaṁ rakkhāvaraṇaguttiṁ saṁvidahati antojanas-

mim . . . . khattiyesu anuyantesu (? *anuyuttesu*) *balakyāasmim brāhmaṇagahapatikesu negamajānapadesu samaṇabrāhmaṇesu migapakkhīsu.* [1]

"Who is, Venerable Sir, the king of the king? Dharma, O Bhikkhus, is the king of the king, said the Blessed One. Here, O Bhikkhus, it is depending on *dharma* (the law of truth and righteousness) honouring, respecting and revering it, doing homage to it, hallowing it, being himself the standard-bearer of *dharma*, the living symbol of *dharma*, and acknowledging sovereignty of *dharma* that the king, overlord, the virtuous and rightful monarch, provides the right watch and rightful protection for his own people, for the army, for the nobles, for vassals, for Brahmins and householders, for town and country-dwellers, for the *religieux*, and for beasts and birds."

It is characteristically observed by the translator of the *Cakkavattisīhanāda-sutta* that "the whole passage in the Pāli is a striking outburst on the superiority of right over might." [2]

That the above idea of *dharma* recognises the superiority of right over might is beyond all doubt. But the principle of righteousness is far more than the mere sense of right or that of duty. The above idea of *dharma* implies that there should not be any right or duty which is imposed from outside. An element of fatigue, dissatisfaction or vexation of spirit is apt to be there when one is to function under such a pressure from without or such an obsession within. The idea of *dharma* is such that there should be the fulfilment of the whole duty of a man as man according to law, according to custom, according to the sense of right, good and happiness but no feeling of tedium or dissatisfaction or vexation of spirit. The whole course of human duty, to oneself, one's people, one's fellow-beings and one's fellow-creatures, is to flow spontaneously from within, out of an inner urge or innate sense without causing vexation or exasperation of spirit. It is indeed such an idea of *dharma* as Aśoka sought to inculcate in so many of his edicts, and inscriptions.

Dharma is something to take one's stand on, [3] something to

---

[1] *Anguttara*, III, pp. 149—50; cf. *Dīgha*, III, p. 61.

[2] *Dialogues of the Buddha*, pt. III, p. 62, fn. 1.

[3] Cf. Aśoka's R.E. IV: *dhaṁmamhi tisṭaṁto*.

adhere to, to abide by, to act in conformity with [1] in all spheres of existence, action, expression or importance for progressive relation of all desired or desirable ends of life. It carries with it the assumption or intuition or recognition or representation of some sort of an order (*niyāmatā*), capacity to hold good (*ṭhititā*), explicability in terms of causality (*idapanayatā*), and causal efficiency (*arthakriyākāritā*). It may stand for any order or system whether of reality or of nature, or of society, or of morality or of thought, or of faith, or of spirit. According to Buddhism, *dharma* broadly involves the conception of five orders (*niyāmas*): *utu* (caloric, chemical, physical), *bīja* (germinal, genital, biological); *kamma* (functional, socio-moral, legal, ethical), *citta* (mental, psychical, psychological); and *dhamma* or *kāraṇa* (logical, dialectical, schematic, metaphysical). [2] The principle, the mode, the method, the facts, the data, the result, in short, all that go to constitute an order or system go by or come under the name of *dharma*.

It is interesting to note that in Indian literature the word *dharma* is conveniently employed together not only with *satya* (Pāli *Sacca*) but also with such words as *artha* (Pāli *attha*), *nyāya* (Pāli *naya*), *yukti* (Pāli *yutti*), *tarka* (Pāli *takka*), *sīla*, *sama*, *vinaya*, *paṭipadā*, or the like, evidently to represent two different aspects of one and the same idea, fact, doctrine or system. In each instance the two's are so juxtaposed as to suggest that one stands as a complement to the other. *Dhammañ ca atthañ ca anusāsi* (administered justice and advantage) is an oft-recurring phrase in the Jātakas. [3] *Dharma*, *Artha*, *Kāma*, and *Mokṣa* constitute the four ends of the Brahmanical system. As for the correlation between *dharma* and *yukti* (which is but another term for *nyāya* and *tarka*) it is definitely enjoined in Raghunandana's *Prāyaścittatattva* (*Brihaspativacana* quoted) that *dharma* declines if it is judged without *yukti* (reasoning). [4] Here reasoning is no more than a reasonable mode of exposition or interpretation which is in conformity with the authority, whether that authority is the *Veda* or the *Tripiṭaka*. In other words,

---

[1] Cf. Aśoka's P.E. VII: *dhammānupaṭipatī anupaṭipajaṁtu*, R.E. X: *dhaṁmavataṁ anuvidhiyatu*.

[2] *Sumaṅgalavilāsinī*, II, 432.

[3] *Jātaka*, Vol. II, 105, *Atthadhammānusāsaka*.

[4] *Yuktihīna-vicāre tu dharmahāniḥ prajāyate*.

yukti is just a ratiocinative means establishing a harmonious link with that which is accepted as the final authority.[1] According to the traditional *yukti* of India, *dharma* is not only that which is in accordance with the established custom or the accepted authority but also that which is lawful, judicious and equitable. *Rajje patiṭṭhāya dhammena samena rajjaṃ kāresi* "Having been established in sovereignty, he governed his kingdom according to law and equity. The same remarks hold true of the Pāli idiom *dhamma-cariyā sama-cariyā*, 'the practice of *dhamma*, the practice of *sama*," *dhamma* and *sama* being in conformity, harmony or consistency with each other.

With regard to the correspondence between *dharma* and *śīla*, we may read in Aśoka's R. E. IV : *dhaṁmamhi sīlamhi tisṭaṁto dhaṁmaṁ anusāsisaṁti*, taking their stand on *dharma* (principle of righteousness, law, piety and morality) and *sīla* (moral conduct) they will administer *dharma*, impart instructions on it." Here *dharma* and *śīla* are to stand in conformity with each other. To say *dhaṁmamhi sīlamhi tisṭaṁto* is the same as to say *dhamme ṭhito*; cf. *Makhādevasutta* (*Majjhima Nikāya*, II, p. 74): *Makhādevo nāma dhammiko dhammarājā dhamme ṭhito dhammaṁ carati brāhmaṇagahapatikesu negamesu c'eva jānapadesu ca uposathañ ca upavasati*. This goes to show that *dharma* itself is the basis or foundation of both *dharma* and *śīla* that are to be fulfilled in practice.

Similarly when Buddha's system as a whole is intended to be meant the term *dharma* or *śāsana* is used and where it is intended to be represented in its two aspects, theoretical and practical, we have the use of two terms *dharma* and *vinaya* (Doctrine and Discipline) instead of one — the *dharma*. *Imasmiṁ dhamma-vinaye* is the same expression as *imasmiṁ dhamme* or *imasmiṁ sāsane*. As for the intended conformity or harmony between the two aspects of Buddha's system as formulated, it is definitely enjoined in the *Dīgha Nikāya*, II, pp. 123, foll.[2] that in establishing a right interpretation of Buddha's word, one must test the soundness of the 'doctrine' aspect in the light of the 'discipline,' and the soundness of the 'discipline' aspect in the light of the 'doctrine'. An interpretation failing to show that one is in conformity with the other, must

[1] Cf. *Netti-pakaraṇa*, *yuttihāra*, pp. 21 foll.

[2] Cf. *Netti-pakaraṇa*, p. 21:

Tāni padabyañjanāni sutte otārayitabbāni, vinaye sandassayitabbāni dhammatāyaṁ upanikkhipitabbāni. Dhammatāyaṁ-Paṭiccasamuppāde.

be rejected as unacceptable. In the case of each Indian system the two aspects are taken together to be its proper representation. So one reads in the *Mahāniddesa*, p. 287: *'parassa ve dhammaṁ anānujānan ti parassa dhammaṃ diṭṭhiṃ paṭipadaṁ maggaṁ anānujānanto.* According to this text, *dhamma* which is the same as *diṭṭhi* (doctrinal viewpoint) and *paṭipadā* which is the same as *magga* (practical viewpoint) are just two sides of one and the same *dhamma*.

The *dharma* is "that which is intuited, or directly sensed or perceived." It is "that which is conceived in thought, represented to oneself, formulated for the satisfaction of the thinker himself." It is also "that which is proclaimed, publicly stated, promulgated in a particular form or fashion, or formulated in the interest of those for whom it is intended." 'That which is intuited, or directly sensed or perceived is either of the nature of reality, or of the material world, or of the mental world, or of the physical world, or of the moral world, or of the intellectual world, or of the spiritual world." "That which is conceived in thought, represented to oneself, formulated for the satisfaction of the thinker himself is the form of solution of the problem which engaged the thinker or contemplative." And "that which is proclaimed, publicly stated, etc., is the nature of criticism of the solution of the problem or problems offered by others as well as of the new direction to all human pursuits." The *dharma* of the second kind is to be in conformity with that of the first, and that of the third is to be in conformity with that of the second, and ultimately with that of the first. Thus indeed one may appreciate the interpretation of the Mahāyāna doctrine of Trikāya, "the three modes of cognition, the successive stages of manifestation, or the three forms of expression of the nature of *dharma* — the *dharmatā*." We read in the *Saṁyutta Nikāya* Vol. II, p. 25:

Uppādā vā Tathāgatānam anuppādā vā Tathāgatānaṁ ṭhitā va sā dhātu dhammaṭhitatā dhammaniyāmatā idappaccayatā. Taṁ Tathā gato abhisambujjhati abhisameti, abhisambujjhitvā abhisametvā ācikkhati deseti paññāpeti paṭṭhapeti vivarati vibhajati uttānīkaroti 'passathāti' cāha.

Mrs. Rhys Davids renders this: "Whether there be an arising of Tathāgatas, or whether there be no such arising, this nature of things just stands, this causal status, this causal orderliness, the relatedness of this to that. Concerning that the Tathāgata is fully enlightened, that he fully understands. Fully enlightened, fully understanding he declares it, teaches it, reveals it, sets it forth, manifests, explains, makes it plain, saying "Behold." [1]

Thitā va sā dhātu. "The element which is in itself, in its own inherent right, independently of all thought or interpretation." This is what is called *dharmatā, tathatā, śūnyatā* or *paurāṇadharmasthititā* (as in the *Laṅkāvatāra Sūtra*). [2]

According to Mrs. Rhys Davids, this involves the conception of "a world-cosmos, wherein cause and effect grinds its way, a cosmodicy rather than a theodicy, an infinite mechanism started none knows when, or how, or to what end." [3]

On the same ground some of the early Buddhist schools of thought (the Pubbaseliya and the Mahisāsaka, according to Buddhaghosa) declared *paṭiccasamuppāda* to be *asaṅkhata*, uncreated by thought, the uncompounded, while the exponent of Theravāda objected to the treatment of *paṭiccasamuppāda* as *asaṅkhata*. *Nibbāna* is *asaṅkhata* with the Theravāda as with the rest of the schools. Thus to regard *paṭiccasamuppāda* as *asaṅkhata* is to admit two *asaṅkhatas* which one could not reasonably do. The decision arrived at in the Mahāyāna system is that *Paṭiccasamuppāda* and *Nibbāna* are essentially one and the same reality. But is *paṭiccasamuppāda* 'dependent origination,' when taken in the sense of *paurāṇa-dharmasthitatā*? The term *pratītyasamutpāda* is employed evidently in this very sense in the opening verse of Nāgārjuna's *Mādhyamika-kārikā*.

Dr. E. J. Thomas observes: "Nāgārjuna begins by discussing the nature of causation as expressed in the theory of dependent origination (*pratītyasamutpāda*) of the causal formula. Dependent origination is said to be characterised by being (1) without cessation, (2) without origination, (3) without cutting off, (4) not eternal, (5) not one, (6) not differentiated, (7) without coming, (8) without going. Its interpretation as a series of causes and effects is entirely rejected". [4]

With Dr. Barua "Nāgārjuna's *pratītyasamutpāda* is the element

---

[1] *The Book of the Kindred Sayings*, II, p. 21.

[2] *Laṅkāvatāra-sūtra*, edited by Nanjio.

[3] *Buddhism* by Mrs. Rhys Davids, revised ed. p. 87

[4] History of Buddhist Thought, p. 219.

of reality [1] which is in itself, in its own inherent right, independently of all thought or interpretation. It is just a 'novelty' as intuited at each moment, either in immediate continuity or at uniform intervals (*anantara, samanantara*), that is to say, a *khaṇa-paccuppanna dhamma*. The novelties are introduced as causally induced factors, or even as links in a chain of dependent origination. It is thus in the sequence of novelties as noted that lies the ground of the theory of causation. The novelty is one thing, the sequence another. The sequence from the viewpoint of the observer is one thing, the causal succession of antecedents and consequents from the viewpoint of the thinker, — another. Upon the whole, the element of reality is the ultimate point of reference of each thought, without differentiation or characterisation."

The *dharmakāya* is to Theravāda, and generally to Hīnayāna, the body of doctrine, the doctrine taught by the Buddha. We read in the *Milindapañha*, p. 73:

'*Dhammakāyena pana kho mahārāja sakkā Bhagavā nidassetum dhammo hi mahārāja Bhagavatā desito.*'

„It is possible, O king, to manifest the Master by the body of the doctrine. The doctrine is taught, O king, by the Master."

The *Dharmakāya* is to Mahāyāna the *dharmatā* the *tathatā*, the *śūnyatā*, the *paurāṇadharmasthititā*, i.e., the element of reality in itself. In other words, this *dharma* or *dharmakāya* is the most essential point in all that is taught by the Buddha. Accordingly we read in the *Saṃyutta nikāya*, Vol. II, p. 267, Vol. V, p. 407:

"*te suttantā Tathāgata-bhāsitā gambhīrā gambhīratthā lokuttarā suññatapaṭisaṁyuttā.*" "Those discourses that are uttered by the Tathāgata, are profound, deep in meaning, and concerned with *suññatā.* "

Suññatā is just another term for *dhammatā, tathatā, dhammaṭhititā.*

The *dharma* which is to be behind, before, and all along thought, action or expression is significantly characterised as *purāṇa* (the most ancient), *śāśvata*, or *sanātana* (eternal). The discovery of the nature of *dharma*, understood in this sense, is compared by the

[1] Cf. *I.H.Q.*, Vol. X, No. 4, p. 758, where Prof. Stcherbatsky observes: "the *dharmas* are not things but elements of things. That the conception of *dharma* is the basic conception of Buddhism is most clearly and pregnantly expressed by the Buddhists themselves in their old *Credo* — "*ye dharmā hetuprabhavāḥ.*"

Buddha to the discovery of an old, buried and forgotten city. So we read in the Pāli *Nagara-sutta* (*Saṁyutta Nikāya*, II. 105—106):

Seyyathāpi bhikkhave puriso araññe pavane caramāno passeyya purāṇam maggaṁ purāṇañjasaṁ pubbakehi manussehi anuyātaṁ || so tam anugaccheyya tam anugacchanto passeyya purāṇaṁ nagaraṁ purāṇaṁ rājadhāniṁ pubbakehi manussehi ajjhāvutthaṁ.

"Just as if, Brethren, a man faring through the forest, through the great wood, should see an ancient path, an ancient road traversed by men of former days. And he should go along it, and going along it he should see an ancient city, an ancient prince's domain, wherein dwelt men of former days."

Next in the *Dhammapada*, Yamakavagga, Verse 5:

Na hi verena verāni sammantīdha kudācanaṁ
Averena ca sammanti esa dhammo sanantano.

"Hatred does not cease by hatred. Enmity ceases by amity. This is the good old rule."

Thirdly, in Aśoka's M.R.E. (Siddāpur): *Esā porāṇā pakiti, dīghāvuse ca esa, hevaṁ esa kaṭiviye.*

"Such is the most ancient nature, that which is of long standing thus indeed (in conformity with that) this should be done."

H'esā pi aṁtevāsīsu yathārahaṁ pavatitaviye yārisā porāṇā pakiti, yathārahaṁ yathā iyaṁ ārokaṁ siyā (Yerraguḍi).

"The same should also be propounded as far as possible to the resident pupils according to the good old rule, so that this (noble tradition) will remain unimpaired" [1].

And fourthly, in the *Bhagavadgītā*, XIV, V. 27:

"*Śāśvatasya ca dharmasya sukhasyaikāntikasya ca.*"

The Pāli expression corresponding to Aśoka's *porāṇā pakiti* is *porāṇiyā-pakati*. The *pakati* or *pakiti* (Sk. *prakṛti*) is no other than another term for *dharma*. The *Sona-Nanda-Jātaka* (Fausböll, No. 532) which embodies a teaching almost literally similar to that in Aśoka's Edicts contains, among others, the following two *gāthās* setting forth the ancient or eternal nature of *dharma*:

Kulavaṁsaṁ mahārāja porāṇaṁ parihāpayaṁ
Adhammacārī jeṭṭhesu nirayaṁ so upapajjati.
Ye ca dhammassa kusalā porāṇassa disampati
Cārittena ca sampannā na te gacchanti duggatiṁ.

[1] The text read and translated by B. M. Barua in *I.H.Q.*, Vol. VII, pp. 118, 120.

According to the first *gāthā*, the *adharmacārī* is one who abandons one's respectful duty to one's elder brothers and others in accordance with the time-honoured tradition of household life.

According to the second *gāthā*, the virtuous man is he who effectually conforms to the ancient tradition, — the established custom.

The gloss adds that here *dhamma* is the *paveṇi-dhamma*, the *dharma* which has held good by continued tradition, — the precedent.

In dealing with the seven essential conditions of welfare of a nation (or of an order or institution) the Buddha definitely lays down:

Yāvakīvañ ca .... appaññattaṁ na paññāpessanti, paññattaṁ na samucchindissanti, yathā paññatte porāṇe .... dhamme vattissanti vuddhi yeva .... pāṭikaṅkhā no parihānī ti. (*Mahāparinibbāna suttanta, Dīgha,* II).

"So long the members of a nation (so of an order or institution) will not introduce that which is not established according to custom, will not destroy that which is established according to custom, and will abide by the good old rule, so long they may be expected to prosper, and not to decline.

In explaining *porāṇe vajji-dhamme* in this text Buddhaghosa speaks of a *paveṇi-potthaka* (Book of Precedents) among the Vṛjis from which guidance was to be taken in deciding all cases. (Vide B. C. Law's *Some Kṣatriya Tribes of Ancient India.* p. 103; Rhys Davids, *Buddhist India*, p. 22).

Thus it may be shown that *purāṇa* or *sanātana* is that which has held good for a long time, that which has been adhered through many ages, that which has, therefore, become a normal state of things, a normal course of life. The normal implies a 'norm' (that which ought to be done or not done), as well as a normal state of the body, mind or morale of a person which enables him to respond to the norm, and to abide by it.

The normal carries with the idea of universal, that which is or may be normally expected of all under a similar set of circumstances.

Sabbeh'eva piyehi manāpehi nānābhāvo vinābhāvo aññathābhāvo 'taṁ kut' ettha .... labbha? 'Yan taṁ jātam bhūtaṁ saṅkhatam palokadhammaṁ tam pana napalujjati, n'etaṁ ṭhānaṁ vijjati.[1]

[1] *Dīgha Nikāya*, Vol. II, p. 158.

"The separation, departure from, the otherness of existing relation with all who are dear and beloved (is a normal way of happening), how can it then be possible to obtain that which is born, has come-to-be, is created and of a nature to disappear will not disappear? There is no ground for such an expectation."

That which is the most ancient in time is the most immediate in experience.[1] It is something which is proved and therefore approved by the wise, and each right-minded individual is normally expected to respond to it. There is no sphere or existence of activity without *dharma*. Birth (*jātidhammo*), decay (*jarā-dhammo*), and the rest are phenomena that normally occur in the natural order, and there are persons or beings who are subject to them. Eating, sleeping procreating, etc., are phenomena that normally occur in the order of life. There are *kula-dharma*, *jñātidharma*, *mitradharma*, *rājadharma*, *strīdharma*, *puruṣadharma*, and the rest, each being normal expression of human nature in the shape of duty in respect of the family, the kinsmen, friendship, kingship, and the like in the social order. So on and so forth.

But to be in *dharma* is to be in one's own element. What one's own element is, depends on one's own feeling, experience, or understanding. There being certain hindrances or obstacles in the way of one's being in one's own element, there being certain other conditions helpful to one's being in one's own element, there being the possibility of removing those obstacles and inducing favourable conditions, a system of training normally involves or comes to prevail in the sphere of education, or a system of practice in the sphere of religion. To be in one's own element in the ultimate sense is to get beyond the known world of cause and effect, *nirvāṇa* or *mokṣa* is that highest state in men's religious experience, in which, alone it is possible to be in one's element in the ultimate sense. *Nirvāṇa* or *vimokṣa* itself is a *dharma* in so far as it is an object of attainment through a life of effort.

In between that which lies behind or lies ahead is the life of effort or pursuit which too is *dharma*. To direct or regulate it there is either a system of society, or a system of education, or a system

[1] "Bṛhadvaiṣṇavatoṣaṇī: *Purāṇaś ca pūrvato nijaiśvaryena vartamāno' pi nava eveti.*" Śrīmadbhāgavata, 10. 14. 23. Cf. Bhāgavatacandrikā: "*Purāṇaḥ purāpi navaḥ.*"

of study, or a system of conduct, or a system of mind, or a system of thought, or a system of faith and worship. It is not only the system as a whole but each part of it goes by the name of *dharma.* For instance, Buddhism as a system of religious thought is called *dharma* or *saddharma*, and each of the thirty-seven main points or terms belonging to that system is also called a *dharma* (*sattatiṁsa bodhipakkhikā dhammā*).

The *Dhammasaṅgaṇī* which is a Buddhist manual of psychological ethics gives an exposition of *dhammas*, classified as moral (*kusala*), immoral (*akusala*) and *avyākata* (indeterminate). These *dhammas* constitute the mental basis of character which finds its expression in conduct or action. Buddhaghosa takes them to mean those mental states which bear their own intrinsic nature (*sabhāva*) [1]. Professor Stcherbatsky has discussed at length precisely in which sense these *dhammas* are regarded as *nissattanijjīva*, the intended distinction being between *nairātmya* (the theory of no-soul) and *nairātma* (the theory of non-soul). [2] According to the opening verse of the *Dhammapada*, mind and all things mental are *dharmas.* [3]

The *Pātimokkha* which is a Buddhist code of monastic discipline contains various rules of conduct, each of which is called a *dhamma*: *pārājikā dhammā, saṅghādisesā dhammā, aniyatā dhammā*, etc.

In the *Cūḷa-Sakuludāyi-Sutta* (*Majjhima Nikāya*, II, p. 32) the term *dhamma* stands for the sequence of facts as experienced or the law of causation or way of happening by a way of cause as formulated:

Dhammaṁ te desessāmi — Imasmiṁ sati idaṁ hoti, imass'uppādā idaṁ upapajjati, etc.

Just as, on the one hand, *dharma* stands for the entire system of sequence, or the chain of dependent origination, so, on the other hand, it stands for each single factor or link, which is accordingly called a *sahetu dhamma, paṭiccasamuppanna dhamma.*

Similarly, it may be shown that *dhamma* stands not only for the entire system of faith, thought or doctrine but for every part or argument or point of it.

---

[1] *Atthasālinī*, p. 63: *Tesaṁ tesaṁ dhammānaṁ sabhāvo vā sāmaññaṁ vā lakkhaṇaṁ nāma.*

[2] *I.H.Q.*, Vol. X, No. 4, p. 743.

[3] *Dhammapada-comy*, I, pp. 22—23; 35—36.

An attempt has recently been made to prove that "the term *dharma* is so devised as to comprehend real, realised and *reality*, actual, actualised and *actuality*, phenomenon, phenomenal and *phenomenality*, matter, material and *materiality*, mind, mental and *mentality*, cause, caused and *causality*, law, legal and *legality*, thought, thinking and *thinkability*, and the like; in short, the entire universe of reality and appearance, truth and opinion, thought and expression, principle and action, in and through which all things and all individuals may realise their being, feel their existence, rise into recognition, move into action or proceed to perfection. That is to say, *dharma* is not only that which was, is or shall be in itself, in its inherent right or in its nature or characteristic form, but that which comes to happen or prevail on account of its inherent force or intrinsic merit or value.

CHAPTER XI

NIBBĀNA

To contemplate the *dhamma* (doctrine) as propounded and promulgated by the Buddha is to contemplate *nibbāna*, while to contemplate the *dhamma* as propounded and promulgated by Aśoka is to contemplate *svaga* (*svarga*), rather *vipula svaga* (unmeasured heavenly joy)[1]. *Nirvāṇa* is the *non plus ultra* of the *dhamma* expounded by the Buddha, the *summum bonum* (*sabbadhammānaṁ uttamaṭṭhena varaṁ*) of Buddhism,[2] the ultimate of all that a Buddha taught or would teach. Thus Buddhism is in essence a proclamation of the truth of *nirvāṇa*, a clear statement of the truth about *nirvāṇa*, a search for *nirvāṇa* (*nibbāna-pariyesanā*), and a tried path leading to *nirvāṇa* (*nibbānagāminī paṭipadā*).[3] The *Netti-pakaraṇa*, which, as a Pāli work of exegesis and analysis, is allowed by tradition to rank in both antiquity and authority with the very oldest of the Buddhist canonical texts, declares to the same effect: —

'*Svākkhāto Bhagavatā dhammo sandiṭṭhiko akāliko ehipassiko opanayiko paccattaṃ veditabbo viññūhi, yad idam madanimmadano pipāsa-vinayo ālayasamugghāto vaṭṭupacchedo suññato atidullabho taṇhakkhayo virāgo nirodho nibbānaṁ*'.[4]

'Well expounded by the Master is the doctrine which bears the desired fruit here and now, which has "Come and See" for its motto, which assuredly leads to the goal, the truth whereof is to be experienced by the wise, each individually for himself, namely, the one which consists essentially in subduing the haughty spirit, the perfect control of thirst, the upsetting of the very storage of creative energy, the arrest of the course of *saṁsāra* as regards the fate of an

---

[1] M.R.E., all copies.

[2] *Khuddakapāṭha-commentary*, p. 193.

[3] *Khuddakapāṭha*, *Ratana-sutta*, V. 12: *dhammavaraṁ adesayi, nibbānagāmiṁ paramaṁ hitāya.*

[4] *Netti*, p. 55.

individual, the rare attainment of the state of the void, the waning out of desire, the dispassionate state, the cessation of all sense of discordance, the *nibbāna.*'

To the very same effect the Buddha is represented in the *Ariya-pariyesana-sutta* as saying: —

'*Nibbānaṁ pariyesamāno ajātaṁ anuttaraṁ yogakkhemaṁ nibbānaṁ ajjhagamaṁ ajaraṁ abyādhiṁ amataṁ asokaṁ asaṅkiliṭṭhaṁ . . . Adhigato kho me ayaṁ dhammo gambhīro duddaso duranubodho santo paṇīto atakkāvacaro nipuṇo paṇḍita-vedanīyo.*' [1]

'In seeking for "salvation" I reached in experience the *nibbāna* which is unborn, unrivalled, secure from attachment, undecaying, unailing, undying, unlamenting and unstained . . . . This condition is indeed reached by me which is deep, difficult to see, difficult to understand, tranquil, excellent, beyond the reach of mere logic, subtle and to be realized only by the wise (each individually for himself).'

The *Vevacana-hāra* of the *Netti* which had served as a literary model for the Pāli lexicon *Abhidhānappadīpikā* catalogues various words or terms, uncritically called synonyms, that bring out different aspects of *nirvāṇa* as conceived and described in early Buddhism [2]. The *Netti-commentary* explains these terms as follows: —

Nirvāṇa is called *asaṅkhata* (uncompounded, absolute) because it is not accounted for by any known causal factor (*na kenaci paccayena saṅkhataṁ*), *ananta* (endless, infinite) because it does not come to an end or knows no extermination (*n'atthi etassa anto vināso*), *anāsava* (stainless) because the influxes of sin have no hold on it (*āsavānaṁ anārammaṇato*), *sacca* (true, real) because it is not of a nature to be other than what it is (*aviparītasabhāvattā*), *pāra* (the other shore), because it makes for the further shore of the ocean of existence through *saṁsāra* (*saṁsārassa paratīrabhāvato*), *nipuṇa* (subtle) because it is accessible only to a subtle cognition as well as because it is in itself of a subtle nature (*nipuṇañāṇa-visayattā sukhuma-sabhāvattā*), *sududdasa* (very difficult to see) because it cannot be apprehended save and except by the instrument of a gradually matured knowledge (*anupacitañāṇasambhārehi daṭṭhuṁ na sakkā*), *ajajjara* (unimpaired) because it is not affected by any

[1] *Majjhima-Nikāya*, I, 167.

[2] *Netti*, p. 55.

process of decay (*uppādajarāhi anabyānatattā*), *dhuva* (immutable) because it is in itself for ever (*cirabhāvena*), *apalokita* (not vanishing) because it does not disappear on account of decay and death (*jarāmaraṇehi apalujjanato*), *anidassana* (invisible) because it is not perceptible to the eye, common or divine (*maṁsacakkhunā dibbacakkhunā ca apassitabbattā*), *nippapañca* (not subject to ramification) because of the absence of the ramibying action of passions (*rāgādipapañcābhāvena*), *santa* (tranquil) because of the total stoppage of the mischievous actions of sin (*kilesābhisaṅkhārānaṁ vūpasamahetutāya*), *amata* (undying) because it is of an immortal nature and it is not liable to disruption (*amatahetutāya bhaṅgābhāvena*), *paṇīta* (excellent) because it is of a supreme kind and it is self-sufficient (*uttamaṭṭhena anappanatthena ca*), *siva* (safe) because there is no effect on it of baneful consequences of sinful deeds (*asivānaṁ kammakilesavipākavaṭṭānaṁ abhāvena*), *khema* (secure) because it is secure from the four fetters (*catūhi yogehi anupaddavabhāvena*), *taṇhakkhaya* (attenuation of desire) because desire is attenuated to nil therein (*taṇhā khīyati ettha*), *acchariya* (wonderful) because it is rarely to be seen even by those who are virtuous (*katapuññehi pi kadācid eva passitabbattā*), *abbhuta* (marvellous) because it is unprecedented (*abhūtapubbattā*), *anītika* (unimpeded) because there is no obstacle in its way (*anantarāyattā*), *anītikadhamma* (not risky) because it is not of a nature to run any risk (*anantarāyabhāvahetuto*), *ajāta* (unborn) because it is not subject to birth (*anibbatti-sabhāvato*), *abhūta* (not subject to becoming, *uppādarahita*) *anupaddava* (undisturbed) because it is not troubled by any disturbing factor (*kenaci anupaddutattā*), *akata* (uncreated) because it is not manipulated by any known cause (*na kenaci paccayena kataṁ*), *asoka* (unlamenting) because there is no sorrow in it (*n'atthi ettha soko*), *visoka* (sorrowless) because there is no cause for sorrow (*sokahetuvigamena*), *anupasagga* (uncomplicated) because it is not complicated by any complication (*kenaci anupasajjitabbattā*), *anupasaggadhamma* (not of a nature to suffer from any complication), *gambhīra* (deep) because it is only within the reach of profound intuition (*gambhīrañāṇagocarato*), *duppassa* (difficult of perception) because it is difficult to perceive, difficult to obtain without the right path (*sammāpaṭipattiṁ vinā passituṁ pattuṁ asakkuṇeyyattā*), *uttara* (transcendental) because it lies beyond the whole of the mundane world (*sabbalokaṁ uttaritvā ṭhitan ti*), *anuttara* (unsurpassed) because there is nothing beyond it (*n'atthi etassa uttaran ti*), *asama* (unequalled) because there is nothing equal to it (*samassa sadisassa abhāvena*), *appaṭisama* (matchless) because there is no counterpart of it (*paṭibhāgābhāvena*), *seṭṭha* (summum bonum, *uttamaṭṭhena*), *jeṭṭha* (supreme) because it is the best thing for praise (*pāsaṁsatamattā*), *leṇa* (habitat) because it is the abode where persons afflicted by wordly sufferings can lie down (*saṁsāradukkhaṭṭhitena letabbato*), *tāna* (protection) because it protects from worldly sufferings (*tato rakkhaṇato*), *araṇa* (hitchless) because there is no hitch in it (*raṇābhāvena*), *anaṅgaṇa* (spotless) because of the absence of any spot (*aṅganābhāvena*), *akāma* (innocent, (*niddosatāya*), *vimala* (unimpure) because all impurities due to passion and the rest are got rid of (*rāgādimalāpagamena*), *dīpa* (island) because it is not subject to innundation on account of the four kinds of flood of sin (*catūhi oghehi anajjhottharaṇīyato*), *sukha* (ease) because of the complete subsidence of the unease of *saṁsāra* (*saṁsāravupasamasukhatāya*), *appamāṇa* (unmeasured, immeasurable) because there is nothing else to measure its worth (*pamāṇakāradhammābhāvato, pamāṇaṁ gahetuṁ etassa na sakkā ti*), *patiṭṭhā* (support) because it is the stand to prevent sinking into dangerous waters of *saṁsāra* (*saṁsārasamudde anosīdanaṭṭhānatāya*), *akiñcana* (having nothing by way of attachment and possession), *rāgādikiñcanābhāvena pariggahābhāvena ca*).

The list of synonyms of *nirvāṇa* in the *Abhidhānappadīpikā* which is substantially the same as that in the *Netti* contains such new terms as follows: —

mukha (*mukhya*, supreme); *arūpa* (incorporeal); *amutta* (*amūrta*, formless, unformed); *saraṇa* (ultimate refuge); *akkhara* (imperishable); *abyāpajjha* (hitchless); *anālaya* (without any stay for desire); *vivaṭṭa* (end of the course of *saṁsāra*); *kevala* (*kaivalya*, a thing in itself, oneness, independence); *apavagga* (*apavarga*, abandonment of the things of the world); *virāga* (*vairāgya*, detachment); *accutapada* (immutable state); *mutti* (liberation); *visuddhi* (purity); *vimutti* (emancipation); *asaṅkhatadhātu* (element of the absolute); *suddhi* (holiness); *nibbuti* (*nirvṛti*, blessedness).

The multiplication of these so-called synonyms of *nirvāṇa* and the philological explanation of them which is, more or less, fancied and fantastic, are of little help in appreciating the Buddhist conception of *nirvāṇa* or in distinguishing the same from the Jaina or the Brahmanical cenception. The only sure and scientific way of attacking the problem of *nirvāṇa* would be to consider it from the different points of view. Our approaches to the subject should not only be logical and mystical, [1] but also historical, eschatological, poetical or popular psychoethical.

Historical Aspect: — The wide popularity of *nirvāṇa* as a distinct term of Indian religious thought is undoubtedly due to the greatest importance attached to it in early Buddhism, by the Buddha, his immediate disciples and his later followers. It is somewhat astonishing that the term occurs nowhere in any of the Vedic or Brahmanical texts that may be definitely assigned to pre-Buddhistic dates. An exception is sought, of course, to be made in favour of Pāṇini's *Aṣṭādhyāyī* accounting grammatically or etymologically for the formation of the word *nirvāṇa* by the aphoristic rule: *Nirvāṇovāte* (8. 2.50.). Pāṇini's date, if it is at all earlier, cannot be far removed from that of the rise of Buddhism. Secondly, it is yet to be ascertained if this particular aphorism belonged actually to Pāṇini's own organon. Even if it did belong, it is still to be seen whether with Pāṇini the word *nirvāṇa* was any more than a popular expression. In popular usage the word *nirvāṇa* was employed either in connection with a burning fire or in connection with a burning lamp, and in both cases it meant nothing but extinction: *pajjotass' eva nibbānaṁ* (*Dīgha*, II, p. 157) like the extinction of a burning fire or lamp; *nibbanti dhīrā yathāyaṁ padīpo* (*Suttanipāta* and *Khuddakapāṭha*, *Ratana-sutta*, V. 14), the wise pass away just in the same way as this burning lamp extinguishes; *nibbuto gini* (*Suttanipāta*, *Dhaniya-sutta*, V, 2), the fire has been extinguished, *nibbuto* standing in contrast to *āhito* meaning 'properly kept up'; *purato aggi nibbāyeyya, ayaṁ me purato aggi nibbuto* (*Majjhima*, I, 487), if this fire before me were to extinguish, if this fire before me were extinguished.

As regards Jaina literature, the term *Nirvāṇa* is met with in the texts of the Āgama, — such authoritative texts as the *Kalpasūtra*, the *Sūtrakṛtāṅga*, the *Uttarādhyayana*, and the rest. But the Jaina

[1] It is mainly from the logical and mystical points of view that Dr. B. M. Barua has considered the question of *nirvāṇa* in his Bombay lecture '*Universal Aspect of Buddhism*'.

predilection, as may be gathered from the Jinakalpa section of the *Kalpasūtra*, is to employ the term *nirvāṇa* to denote the final liberation of the human soul (*mokṣa*) from all kinds of bondage, which is not possible before the demise of a Tīrthaṅkara. In other words, with the Jainas, *nirvāṇa* is the same term as *parinirvāṇa*. The nine main terms (*nava-tattva*) of Jainism which became current and widely known as early as the time of the Buddha, include *nijjarā* and *mokkha*.[1] The *Kalpa-sūtra* describes Mahāvīra's demise in these terms: 'Mahāvīra died, went off, quitted the world, cut asunder the ties of birth, old age and death; became a *siddha*, a Buddha, a *mukta*, a maker of the end (to all misery), finally liberated, freed from all pains' (*Jaina Sūtras*, S.B.E., Part I, p. 264).

It would be going against historical truth to suppose that *nirvāṇa* as a final term of Indian religious thought was altogether an innovation or invention on the part of the Buddha. The very first discourse in the *Majjhima-nikāya*, appropriately called *Sabbadhamma-mūlapariyāya*, clearly indicated that already at the time of the rise of Buddhism, *nirvāṇa* came to be recognized as the final term or 'ultimate category' of Indian religious thought. In this most important discourse, the Buddha is recorded as distinguishing his own attitude towards *nirvāṇa* from that which had passed as the prevalent attitude. One may readily agree to think that 'this difference in the two attitudes or thought-positions implies a difference in two conceptions or notions: *nirvāṇa* from the cosmological or ontological point of view, and *nirvāṇa* from the logical or epistemological point of view, the difference being set forth in the original text as follows:

(1) *Idha bhikkhave assutavā puthujjano .... Nibbānaṁ nibbānato sañjānāti, nibbānaṁ nibbānato saññatvā nibbānaṁ maññati, nibbānasmiṁ maññati, nibbānato maññati, nibbānaṁ me ti maññati, nibbānaṁ abhinandati*; (M.N., I, p. 4).

2) *Tathāgato pi bhikkhave arahaṁ sammāsambuddho .... nibbānato abhijānāti, nibbānaṁ nibbānato abhiññāya nibbānaṁ na*

---

[1] *Devadaha-sutta*, *Majjhima-Nikāya*, II, p. 214:
'*purāṇānaṁ kammānaṁ tapasā vyantibhāvā, navānaṁ kammānaṁ akaraṇā āyatiṁ anavassavo, āyati anavassavā kammakkhayo, kammakkhayā dukkhakkhayo, dukkhakkhayā vedanākkhayo, vedanākkhayā sabbaṁ dukkhaṁ nijjiṇṇaṁ bhavissati.*'
Here the term *nijjarā* occurs instead *nijjiṇṇa*.

maññati, nibbānasmiṁ na maññati, nibbānato na maññati, nibbānaṁ me ti na maññati, nibbānaṁ nābhinandati. (*M.N.*, I, p. 6).

This may be taken to suggest two different modes of thinking, one, the Brahmanist mode, by which was developed the idea of *Brahmanirvāṇa*, and the other, the Buddha's mode, by which was developed the Buddhist idea of *nirvāṇa*. With the Brahmanist of all ages *nirvāṇa* is *Brahma-nirvāṇa*, whether Brahman is *saguṇa* or *nirguṇa*. That is to say, with the Brahmanist thinker, precisely as with the Jaina, the problem of *nirvāṇa* is approached from the point of view of *ātman*, whilst with the Buddha or Buddhist thinker the approach is from the view-point of *anātman*. [1].

Eschatological Aspect: — The belief already gained ground among the people of India at the time of the rise of Buddhism that true salvation of man consists in evolving into an eternal personality exhausting all possibilities of rebirth, — of reappearing in the mother's womb as they would put it. [2] The whole chain of reasoning is: To be subject to birth is to be subject to decay and death. The world of life is so ordained that there is no escape from decay and death for one who has been brought into existence by the natural process of creation, — by the parental union in the case of all higher forms of earthly beings. [3] The very possibility of such an escape is denied by the daily experience of things or events happening around and at all times. [4] Even a *Buddha* or *Tathāgata* cannot escape it in spite of his universally admitted and unrivalled greatness and perfection. [5] And *Saṁsāra* for an individual is nothing in

---

[1] *Vide Laṅkāvatāra-sūtra.*

[2] *Metta-sutta, Khuddakapāṭha* and *Suttanipāta*: *na hi jātu gabbhaseyyaṁ punar eti.*

[3] *Majjhima*, I, p. 266: *Idha mātāpitaro ca sannipatitā honti, mātā ca utunī hoti, gandhabbo ca paccupaṭṭhito hoti .... evaṁ tiṇṇaṁ sannipātā gabbhassāvakkanti hoti.*

[4] *Mahāparinibbāna-suttanta, Dīgha*, II, p. 158: *yaṁ taṁ-jātaṁ bhūtaṁ saṅkhataṁ palokadhammaṁ taṁ māpalujjiti n'etaṁ ṭhānaṁ vijjati.*

Cf. The *Mohamudgara* verse:

Yāvaj jananaṁ tāvan maraṇam,
tāvaj jananī-jaṭhare śayanaṁ.

[5] So *Brahmā Sahampati* declares (*Dīgha*, II, p. 157):

Sabb'eva nikkhipissanti bhūtā loke samussayaṁ
yathā etādiso Satthā loke appaṭipuggalo.

common parlance but the painful necessity of undergoing the repeated process of birth and death — of passing through the cycles of birth and death, running in the course of transmigration of soul, [1] or finding somehow the concatenation of individual existence through the repeated natural process of birth and death. [2]

It is the consciousness of the 'contingent character' of *saṁsāra*, the world of life and existence, and the bitter experience of its 'unpleasantness' or 'unsatisfactory sequel' that is at the back of the religious quest of a permanent ground of existence and experience, — a permanent feature or element of reality, some sort of an Absolute. So Buddha is represented as saying: 'Having been myself subject to the contingency of birth and experienced its unpleasantness, I sought for *Nirvāṇa* which is without such contingency, — which is unsurpassed and secure from all worldly yoke, and obtained it. Subject to the contingency of decay, the contingency of disease, death, sorrow, and sin, I sought for *Nirvāṇa* which is without such and such contingency, — which is unsurpassed and secure from all worldly yoke, and obtained it. The knowledge with the vision arose: 'Sure is my final emancipation, this is the last birth, there is no longer the 'possibility of rebirth'. Then this thought occurred to me: 'I have reached this element of things which is deep, difficult to see, difficult to understand, tranquil, excellent, not within the access of mere logic, subtle and to be experienced only by the wise, each for himself. The multitudes find delight in the home, they are attached to the home' and rejoice over it. It is difficult indeed for them to apprehend this position (of *saṁsāra*), namely, the causal determination of all occurrences in fact, — of all becoming, — to apprehend also this position (of Nirvāṇa), namely, that it is the subsidence of all predisposition towards the form of creation, the relinquishment of all ideas of belongings, the extinction of desire, the dispassion, the cessation, the ultimate. [3]

Even the Buddha himself is recorded as saying (*Majjhima* I, p. 82): *Ahaṁ kho pana etarahi jiṇṇo vuddho mahallako addhagato vayo anuppatto, asītiko me vayo vattati.*

[1] The idea is Brahmanical as well as Jaina.

[2] The Buddhistic way of expressing it.

[3] *Majjhima*, I, p. 167: *So kho ahaṁ attanā jātidhammo samāno jātidhamme ādinavaṁ viditvā ajātaṁ anuttaraṁ yogakkhemaṁ nibbānaṁ pariyesamāno*

The authoritative utterance or verbal testimony (*aññā, ājñā*) of all the Early Buddhist Brethren and Sisters is to this effect: 'I have lived the holy life, done all that I was to do, and am now free from all attachment. Completely destroyed is the cause of birth through cycles of existence, there is no longer the possibility of any re-birth'. [1]

But is this a genuine feeling felt in the innermost depth of one's being or self-consciousness, or an actuality? The question was raised by many an interested inquirer in Buddha's time, and it still remains: What happens to a Tathāgata (Perfect Man) after death? Does he continue to exist or does he cease to exist? Does he both exist and not exist, or does he neither exist nor not exist? [2]

Buddha felt constrained to remain silent whenever such an inquiry was pressed. He was always reluctant to commit himself to any statement in reply to any of the above four queries. The real reason is that he was not prepared to admit any of the questions, — to entertain the inquiry in that form. With the inquirers, however, those were the question of questions, the question that vitally concerned them.

In the *Cūḷa-Māluṅkya-Sutta* (*Majjhima*, I, p. 432), Māluṅkyaputta is advised by Buddha to treat his *avyākata* (point in regard to which he did not commit himself to any one-sided statement whatsoever) as *avyākata*, and his *vyākata* as *vyākata*. The inquiry referred to above is to be counted among Buddha's *avyākatas*. Seeing that another inquirer, *Aggi-Vacchagotta*, got rather puzzled than enlightened when he was told in all stages of inquiry. 'Vaccha,

---

ajātaṁ .... ajaraṁ .... abyādhiṁ .... amataṁ .... asokaṁ .... asaṅkiliṭṭhaṁ anuttaraṁ yogakkhemaṁ nibbānaṁ ajjhagamaṁ. Ñāṇaṇ ca pana me dassanaṁ udapādi: akuppā me vimutti, ayam antimā jāti, n'atthi dāni punabbhavo ti. Tassa mayhaṁ etad ahosi: Adhigato kho me ayaṁ dhammo gambhīro duddaso duranubodho santo paṇīto atakkāvacaro nipuṇo paṇḍitavedanīyo .... Ālayarāmāya kho pana pajāya ālayaratāya ālayasammuditāya duddasaṁ idaṁ ṭhānaṁ yadidaṁ idappaccayatā paṭiccasamuppādo, idam pi kho ṭhānaṁ duddasaṁ yadidaṁ sabbasaṇkhārasamatho sabbūpadhipaṭinissaggo taṇhakkhayo virāgo nirodho nibbānaṁ.

[1] *Theragāthā and Therīgāthā: Vusitaṁ brahmacariyaṁ, katakiccaṁ anāsavaṁ. Vikkhīṇo jātisaṁsāro, n'atthi dāni punabbhavo.*

[2] *Majjhima*, I, pp. 426 ff.: *Kin nu kho hoti .... na hoti .... hoti ca na ca hoti .... n'eva hoti na na hoti Tathāgato param maraṇā?*

the inquiry in this form does not suit me, is not fitting (*na upeti*): Buddha felt it necessary to explain his own position thus: —

'Just as it is not possible to know whither the fire is gone which was so long burning before a man after once for all it is extinguished on the exhaustion of all materials of burning, — the fuel, in the same way it is not possible to represent a Tathāgata after he has passed away on the complete exhaustion of all materials of bodily existence and of all prerequisites of representation of an individual as commonly known.' [1]

To say that Buddha attained *parinirvāṇa* (*sambuddho parinibbuto*) is the same as to say in ordinary language that he died (*kālam akari muni*) [2]. In his own words, to attain *parinirvāṇa* is to see 'the fire of life extinguished in that elemental condition of extinction which allows no residuum of possibility for re-ignition' (*anupādisesāyanibbānadhātuyā parinibbuto*). The mannex in which Buddha attained *parinirvāṇa* is said to have been described by *Thera Anuruddha* in the following terms: 'There was then no process of respiration to be noticed in the organism of the great saint whose mind was then unshaken, steadily concentrated that it then was on its peacefulness, when he expired. With an unperturbed mind he did bear the pangs of death. Just as fire extinguishes on the exhaustion of all materials of burning, in the same way his consciousness became completely emancipated'. [3]

In the *Ratana-Sutta*, the Disciples of Buddha who experience or realize the bliss of *nirvāṇa* are praised as personages who 'expire like a burning lamp' (on the exhaustion of oil and wick) [4]. Whilst

[1] *Majjhima*, I, pp. 487—488. The statement is summarized for the sake of brevity: *Yena rūpena . . . . yāya vedanāya . . . . yāya saññāya . . . . yehi saṅkhārehi . . . . yena viññāṇena Tathāgataṁ paññāpayamāno paññāpeyya taṁ viññāṇaṁ Tathāgatassa pahīnaṁ ucchinnamūlaṁ tālāvatthukataṁ anabhāvakataṁ āyatiṁ anuppādadhammaṁ. . . . viññāṇasaṅkhāvimutto kho Vaccha Tathāgato gambhīro appameyyo duppariyogāho seyyathā pi mahāsamuddo, upapajjatī ti na upeti, na upapajjati ti na upeti . . . .*

[2] *Dīgha*, II, p. 157.

[3] *Dīgha*, II, p. 157:

Nāhu assāsa-passāso ṭhitacittassa tādino,
Anejo santim ārabbha yaṁ kālam akarī muni.
Asallīnena cittena vedanaṁ ajjhavāsayi:
Pajjotass' eva nibbāṇaṁ vimokho cetaso ahū ti.

[4] *Nibbanti dhīrā yathāyaṁ padīpo.* (*Khuddakapāṭha*, p. 5).

they live, they live enjoying the bliss of peace obtained without having to pay any price for it [1].

Such is, in short, the Buddhist description of *parinirvāṇa* which is the natural end of life of those gifted men who realize *nirvāṇa* in their present conscious existence (*diṭṭh'eva dhamme*). [2]

With the Jaina, too, *parinirvāṇa* is the last fruit or final consummation of the highest perfection attained by a man or attainable in human life. [3] But with him *parinirvāṇa* is the same term as *nirvāṇa* [4] or *mokṣa* meaning final liberation that comes to pass on the complete waning out or exhaustion of the accumulated strength or force of *karma*.

With the Jaina, however, *nirvāṇa* or *mokṣa* is not a dreadful or terrible term like the Buddhist *parinirvāṇa* which suggests at once an idea of the complete annihilation of individuality of a saint after death by the simile of the total extinction of a burning lamp on the exhaustion of the oil and the wick. So the point is discussed in the Jaina *Mokṣasiddhi*: 'Would you really think (with the Buddhist) that *nirvāṇa* is a process of extinction of human soul which is comparable to the process of extinction of a burning lamp (on the exhaustion of the oil and the wick)? [5] The hearer is advised not to think like that. For with the Jaina *nirvāṇa* is nothing but a highly

---

[1] *Laddhā mudhā nibbutiṁ bhuñjamānā.* (*ibid.*, p. 4).

[2] Cf.

Dīpo yathā nirvṛtimabhyupeto
naivāvaniṁ gacchati nāntarīkṣam,
diśaṁ na kāñcit vidiśaṁ na kāñcit
snehakṣayāt kevalameti śāntim.
Jīvas tathā nirvṛtimabhyupeto
naivāvaniṁ gacchati nāntarīkṣaṁ,
Diśaṁ na kāñcit vidiśaṁ na kāñcit
kleśakṣayāt kevalameti śāntim.

(*Saundarananda Kāvya.*)

[3] *Kalpasūtra* (Jacobi's edition), 120: *Tassa naṁ anuttareṇaṁ nāṇeṇaṁ* .... *daṁseṇaṇaṁ* .... *carittenaṁ* .... *āhaenam* .... *vihārenaṁ* .... *virieṇaṁ* .... *ajjaveṇaṁ* .... *maddaveṇaṁ* .... *lāghavenaṁ* .... *aṇuttarāe muttie guttie tuṭṭhie buddhie, anuttareṇaṁ sava-saṁjamatavasucariyā sovaciya-phala-parinirvāṇa.*

[4] *Kalpasūtra*, 189: *Tasmiṁ samae Mahāvīro nivvuo. Nivvuo* = Pali *parinibbuto.*

[5] *Mannasi kiṁ dīvassa ca nāso nivvāṇaṁ assa jīvassa?* quoted in the *Abhidhāna-rājendra sub voce Nibbāṇa.*

special or transcendental condition of human soul, in which it remains eternally and absolutely, free from passion, hatred, birth, decay, disease, and the like, because of the complete waning out of all causes of *dukkha.* [1]

The *Milindapañha* definitely says that after the attainment of *parinirvāṇa* the Buddha is no longer in that condition in which he is able to receive any offering made in his honour, though the offering itself as an act of worship is not fruitless on that account, so far as the worshipper is concerned. Thus the Buddhist description of Buddha's *parinirvāṇa* leaves no room for the popular belief in the possibility of resurrection of the bodily form or even the spiritual form, of a saint. [2] Is it, nevertheless, a complete cessation of personality, even if that personality is made up of pure consciousness? According to the *Laṅkāvatāra-Sūtra*, there is then *lakṣaṇa-nirodha* (cessation of all signs of manifestation), but no *prabandha-nirodha* (cessation of process of *vijñāna* in its own pure or transcendental mode). [3]

In all stages of evolution of religious thought in India the description of the ultimate goal of the higher path of religious effort carried with it the dread of extinction of the individual after death. In the opinion of such ancient law-givers as Baudhāyana and Āpastamba, the *devayāna* leading the traveller by an onward journey to the pure realm of infinity beyond the solar region led really but to the funeral ground *śmaśāna*, and those who travel by that path 'alone', in disregard of *pitṛyāna* become ultimately 'dust and perish' (*rajo bhūtvā dhvaṁsate*). [4]

Ṛṣi Yājñavalkya's statement of the fate of the soul after man's death caused puzzlement to the simple-minded Maitreyī: 'Verily I say unto thee the soul is complete in itself, within and without. As a mass of intelligence (or consciousness), it emerges out of these (five) elements and loses its form of manifestation with their dis-

---

[1] *Sato vidyamānasyā jīvasya viśiṣtā kācid avasthā. Kathaṁbhūtā? Rāga-dveṣa-janmajāra-rogādi duḥkhakṣaya-rūpā.*

[2] Note the description of emergence of an effulgent miniature form of the sage Śarabhaṅga out of burning fire to which he offered himself as an oblation. *Vide Rāmāyaṇa, Araṇyakāṇḍa.*

[3] *Vide Laṅkāvatāra-Sūtra* (Nanjio's edition).

[4] Barua, *History of pre-Buddhistic Indian Philisophy*, pp. 247—249.

integration. There is no cognizance of it after man's death'.[1] He offered an explanation, the tenor of which went to establish that as the soul after man's death passes beyond all duality, it does not admit of any representation in the current terms of thought. It then becomes the whole or infinity, and the whole or infinity is its own description.[2]

Similarly Buddha's persistent reluctance to answer any of the four questions put to him regarding the fate of the Tathāgata after death caused puzzlement to his interlocutor, Aggi-Vacchagotta.[3] Buddha, too, offered an explanation, the purport of which was to indicate that the condition of Tathāgata after *parinirvāṇa* was incapable of description in all convenient terms of description: *rūpa, vedanā, saññā, saṅkhāra and viññāṇa.*

An illuminating description of the state or condition of existence reached by a person on the attainment of *parinirvāṇa* is met with in the *Udāna,* (p. 9), and it has been put into the mouth of Buddha himself. The same is quoted below in the original with its translation: —

'*Yattha āpo ca paṭhavī tejo vāyo na gādhati,*
Na tattha sukkā jotanti ādicco na ppakāsati.
Na tattha candimā bhāti tamo tattha na vijjati.
Yadā ca attan' āvedi muni monena brāhmaṇo,
atha rūpā arūpā ca sukhadukkhā pamuccatī ti.'

'Where water, earth, heat and air do not find footing, there no light burns and the sun does not shine, the moon does not shed her radiant beams and darkness does not exist there. When a sage who is a brāhmaṇa has realized the truth by silent concentration, then he becomes free from form and formlessness, happiness and suffering.'

Poetical Aspect: — *Nirvāṇa* or *Parinirvāṇa* as an abstract idea, or as a transcendental sphere of man's existence, cannot have a

---

[1] *Bṛhad Ār. Upa.*, Chap. II, Vs. 12 and 13: *ātmānantaro bāhyaḥ kṛtsaḥ prajñānaghan* (= *vijñānaghana*) *evaitebhyo bhūtebhyaḥ samutthāya tānyevānuvinaśyati na pretya saṃjñāstīyare bravīmīti hovāca Yājnavalkyaḥ. Sā hovāca: Atraiva mā Bhagavān mohāntam āpipipanna.*

[2] *Bṛhad Ār. Upa.*, Chap. II, 14: *Yatra hi dvaitam iva bhavati taditara itaram abhivadati . . . . vijānāti yatra tvasya sarvam ātmaivābhut tat kena kam śṛṇuyāt . . . ?*

[3] *Majjhima,* I, p. 487: *Etthāhaṃ bho Gotama aññānaṃ āpādiṃ, sammoham āpādim.*

true and lasting appeal to the popular mind which demands for its satisfaction the conception and description of someting more positive and tangible. The process of poetry and myth becomes, therefore, active, to create that something more positive and tangible, — a paradise in its highest glory. The beginning of this process of poetry and myth can be clearly traced in a group of verses known by the name of *Accharāgāthā* (*Saṁyutta*, I, *Sagāthavagga*). In these verses Buddhism is described as the safest and fittest vehicle (*yāna*) carrying all men, women, recluses and householders, to *Nirvāṇa* which is the destination. The progress of the Buddhist aspirant towards this goal is poetically described in terms of a noiseless and fearless and steady procession or chariot-march by a straight road and with an unerring aim. [1]

The account of Buddha's Great Decease in the *Mahāparinibbāna-Suttanta* makes it evident that it was too much for average men to brook the idea that a great Buddha, too, failed to overcome death, in spite of his unrivalled greatness and enviable perfection. This fact was dreadful to them as it went to furnish them with the last proof of man's inability to overcome death, of which the whole of sentient creation is mortally afraid. To say that one cannot possibly overcome death after being once in the grip of birth, but one can surely overcome the fear of death, is no answer to the real yearning of their heart. The belief gradually gained ground among certain Buddhists that the Buddhas as superhuman personalities exist in all quarters (*Sabbā disā Buddhā tiṭṭhanti*). [2]

The *Milinda-pañha* gives a realistic hand at the same time exaggerated poetical description of *Dhammanagara* or ideal Buddhist city as it came to prevail within a few centuries after Buddha's demise. [3] Even in a somewhat earlier stage of Buddhist poetic fancy, one has in the Pāli *Apadāna* [4] a charming romantic description of *Buddha-khetta* (The Realm of Buddha) in which all Buddhas, all

---

[1] *Ujuko nāma so maggo abhayā nāma sā disā, ratho akūjano nāma dhammacakkehi saṁyutto.* Cf. *Prākrit Dhammapada*, by Barua and Mitra, p. 18.

[2] *Kathāvatthu*, II, 608.

[3] *Milinda-pañha*, pp. 332—345.

[4] *Apadāna*, I, Verses 29—30: '*Sāvakā buddhe pucchanti buddhā pucchanti sāvake,*
Aññamaññañ ca pucchanti aññamaññañ byākaronti te.
Buddhā Paccekabuddhā ca sāvakā paricārakā
Evaṁ ratisu ramamānā pāsāde 'bhiramanti te.'

Disciples, and all followers and worshippers, find their place. No birth, no death. No sorrow, no lamentation. A ceaseless scene of peaceful worship and religious conversation in the midst of the very best of natural surroundings. A full heart and a serene mind in a world of plenty.

The same process of poetry and myth continued to produce at last the Sanskrit *Sukhāvati-vyūha*, a Mahâyāna work, giving a highly romantic or imaginative description of a Buddhist Paradise, the realm of Amitābha, Amitaprabha. The Sukhāvatī is the infinite world of light, brilliance and effulgence. The Amitābha, as it may be easily guessed, is no other than the Buddha in his infinite glory after his demise, — the *mahāparinibbāna*.

A similar poetic imagery about *nirvāṇa* lingers in the metaphorical expression *nirvāṇanagara* or *nirvāṇapura* which is met with in Buddhaghosa's *Visuddhimagga* and some of the later Jaina works.

Logical Aspect: — If it be assumed that *saṁsāra*, as commonly understood, is something which has the contingency of birth, development and death (*jāta, bhūta, mata*), the inquiry may pertinently arise if there is something else which has no such contingency (*ajāta, abhūta, amata*). This inquiry was once pressed by certain inquirers among Buddha's immediate disciples. When the issue was thus pressed, Buddha gave a reply, the tenor of which went to convince the inquirers that they simply begged the question in pressing such an inquiry The argument indeed was: 'The very fact that you have been striving after that something else which is without such contingency is sufficient to prove that you have been tacitly all believers in its possibility and were you not tacitly believers in its possibility, you would not have cared to strive after it'. [1]

According to Nāgārjuna, *Saṁsāra* and *Nirvāṇa* are two relative ideas, and as such, there can be difference but no absolute distinction between the two (*saṁsārasya ca nirvāṇasya nāsti kiñcit viśeṣatā*). If the significance of one term is dependent on the significance of the other, both stand on the same footing in respect of each other. There cannot be any conception of a relation between the two even in apposition, if there be not a common point of reference which is without differentiation or characterization, and from which

[1] *Udāna*, pp. 80—81.

ultimately each derives its significance. By implication, this common point of reference is no other than *pratītyasamutpāda*, *dharmatā*, *tathatā*, or *śūnyatā*, which is introduced in the very opening verse of Nāgārjuna's *Kārikā*. The *pratītyasamutpāda*, viewed and interpreted as a law of sequence of causal antecedents and consequents, — as causally determined continuity (*santati*), explains the essential nature of *saṁsāra*. The same, viewed and interpreted as 'novelty' (*uppādamatta* [1], *khaṇapaccuppanna* [2]) without any idea of temporal or spatial relation associated with it, expresses the essential nature of *Nirvāṇa* or Infinity. In plain terms, the *pratītyasamutpāda* in its *samutpāda* aspect is *saṁsāra* and the same in its *nirodha* aspect is *Nirvāṇa* [3]. The Canonical authority to be cited in this connection is Buddha's statement in the *Ariyapariyesana-sutta* (*Majjhima Nikāya*, I. p. 167).

By the dialectical process of reasoning employed in the *Mūlapariyāya-Sutta* (*Majjhima*), Buddha sought to show that *Nirvāṇa* cannot but be the final term or last category of thought. If the first sources of knowledge be perception or intuition (*diṭṭha*), tradition (*suta*) and inference (*muta*), all that is derived from these three sources may be comprehended and made significant by the term *viññāta* (the known, i.e. knowledge). The first three terms cannot exhaust the meaning of *viññāta* which is something more than what is comprehended by them, jointly or severally. If *ekatta* (unity) be the next category to express the essential character of knowledge (*viññāta*, the known), yet another category — *nānatta* (plurality) is needed to cover the residual of meaning not covered by *ekatta*. To comprehend the meaning of both *ekatta* (unity) and *nānatta* (plurality), another category is called forth, namely, *sabba* (the all, universality) which is something more in meaning than what is comprehended by both *ekatta* and *nānatta*. Even *sabba* (the intellectual

---

[1] According to Buddhaghosa, *uppādamatta* cannot be a valid interpretation of *paṭiccasamuppāda*. (*Visuddhimagga*, II. p. 519).

[2] For the term, see *Atthasālinī*, pp. 420—1:

Paccuppannaṁ nām' etaṁ tividhaṁ: Khaṇa-, santati-, addhā-, Santati-paccuppannaṁ c'ettha aṭṭhakathāsu āgataṁ, addhā-paccuppannaṁ sutte. Tattha keci khaṇa-paccuppannaṁ cittaṁ cetopariyañāṇassa ārammaṇaṁ hoti ti vadanti. Kiṁ kāraṇā? Yasmā iddhimassa parassa ca ekakkhaṇe cittaṁ uppajjissatī ti idañ ca tesaṁ opammaṁ.

[3] Vide chapter on *Buddhist Conception of Dhamma*.

universality) is in itself inadequate to comprehend the whole of reality which is constituted not only of cognition, but also of volition and feeling, to comprehend all of which yet another category is required, and it is *Nirvāṇa* (the Ideal, Ideality). It is not an experience that one may identify oneself with it or think that either one is *Nirvāṇa*, or one is in *Nirvāṇa*, or one is from *Nirvāṇa*, or *Nirvāṇa* is one's own. [1]

Psychical Aspect: — Here psychical is just another term for mystical. The mystic, as distinguished from *saddhāvimutta* (devotee) or *paññāvimutta* (intellectualist), aspires to be a *Kāyasakkhi* [2] or personal witness to, to be face to face with, to have a direct perception of, to come in immediate contact with, in short, to realize *nirvāṇa* by himself and for himself. It is after such realization that he begins to utter the joy of self-expression (*udānaṁ udāneti*), to give an expression to self-mastery (*aññā*), and to teach the way of realizing *nirvāṇa* to others (*abhiññā sacchikatvā pavedeti*). With him *nirvāṇa* is at once a vision, an experience, a feeling, and a self-state, — the highest, the best, the most real of all that he knows of, thinks of, or speaks of. As an element of experience, it is inalienable, because the wise are to experience, each in himself by himself and for himself (*paccattaṁ viññūhi veditabbaṁ*); it cannot be communicated to others, because its nature, as experienced by each individual, is indescribable in words. The message or personal testimony must be worthy of trust, the individual bearing it must be in a perfectly sound condition of body, mind, intellect, and spirit. The vision of *nirvāṇa* dawns upon consciousness, the realization of *nirvāṇa* is possible in that stage of *samādhi* (trance, self-concentration) which is aptly called *saññāvedayitanirodha*. According to Buddha's claim, this is the ninth stage of *samādhi* reached for the first time by him, one step ahead of eight *samāpattis* (attainments, first stages of *samādhi*) mastered by other contemplatives in India already before his advent. [3] The *Satipaṭṭhāna* is the well-tried grammar to be followed by the aspirant in assuredly reaching and mastering all the nine stages of *samādhi*, the ninth being truly

---

[1] *Majjhima* I, p. 6.

[2] See for the explanation of these terms, Barua's 'Faith in Buddhism' in B. C. Law's *Buddhistic Studies*, pp. 329—349.

[3] *Ariyapariyesana-Sutta*, *Majjhima*, I, pp. 163—6.

called *nirvikalpa* (without any excogitation) and *nirābhāsa* (without any illusion or hallucination). Without going into details here it may suffice to quote the following short but intelligible description of the psychical mode:

'In accordance with the mystical or psychical mode, the process of meditation is to proceed from one plane of experience or one level of consciousness to another. The highest state of trance . . . . reached by Buddha is called *saññā-vedayita-nirodha*. This is a state of trance when outwardly the man who reaches it is as good as dead, [1] there being nothing but warmth (*ussā*) as the sign of life. [2] In this state, a level of consciousness (*citta*) is reached where consciousness is ultimately thrown back on itself, completely void (*suñña*), being devoid of the subject-object relation (*grāhya-grāhaka-bhāva-rahita*).[3] In the same state, a plane of religious experience is reached where there is no longer any longing for this or that object of sense. This is the highest psychical state where consciousness appears to be face to face with reality'. [4]

Ethical Aspect: — The ethical aspect of *nirvāṇa* is too well-known to need much elucidation here [5]. Let it suffice to say that the main ethical term to express the nature of Buddhist *nirvāṇa* (and *à posteriori*, that of Jaina) [6] is *Visuddhi* or Purity. From the ethical point of view, to realise *nirvāṇa* is to attain the highest purity of one's own self, — of one's own nature (*visuddhim attano*). Thus the

[1] When on the eve of the Great Decease, Buddha remained lost in the *samādhi* called *saññāvedayita-nirodha*, Ānanda thought he was already dead and gone. See *Dīgha*, II, p. 156: '*Parinibbuto bhante Anuruddha Bhagavā ti? Na āvuso Ānanda Bhagavā parinibbuto, saññā-vedayitanirodhaṁ samāpanno ti.*

[2] Dr. N. Dutt (*Aspects of Mahāyāna Buddhism and its relation to Hīnayāna.* pp. 129 foll.), has attempted an elaborate description of the *jhāna* and *samādhi* stages, which is not, however, so illuminating and clear and psychological as that in Shwe Zan Aung's Introductory Essay, *Compendium of Buddhist Philosophy*.

[3] *Madhyāntavibhāgasūtrabhāṣyaṭīkā* of *Sthiramati*, Pt. I, p. 10: *Sā ca (Śūnyatā) grāhya-grāhaka-(bhāva)-rahitatā.*

[4] Barua, Bombay Lecture, *Universal Aspect of Buddhism*.

[5] *Childers*, Art. on *Nibbāna* in Dict. of the Pāli Language: *Nibbāna* in the *Pāli-English Dict.* by Rhys Davids; views of Dr. L. Vallee Poussin, Prof. Theodore Stcherbatsky, and Prof. Berriedale Keith about *Nirvāṇa*.

[6] *Sūtrakṛtāṅga*, I, 1, 2, 27 (*Jaina Sūtras*, Part. II, p. 243): 'by purity of the heart one reaches *Nirvāṇa*'.

method of realization of *nirvāṇa* necessarily involves a process of perfect self-examination, self-purification, self-restraint and self-culture. If the experience of *nirvāṇa* consists in the feeling of peacefulness, tranquillity or harmony in the whole of one's being and in the whole of nature by which one is surrounded, it is not possible without the practice of self-alienation from all that is not one's own. Thus the process of a self-alienation involves a method of viewing things as they are (*yathābhūtaṁ, bhūtaṁ bhūtato, ṭhitaṁ ṭhitato*). From one point of view, the twofold ethical end of Buddhism is negative: (1) to keep off the hindrances (*nīvaraṇas*), and (2) to put away the fetters (*saṁyojanas*) or to destroy the *anusayas* (the sinfulness that lies deep in our nature). From another point of view, the end is positive, namely, to attain a perfect healthy condition of self. The rough scheme of self-culture through purity is set forth in the *Rathavinītasutta* (*Majjhima*, I, pp. 147—8) and it includes the following main items for consideration: —

Sīla-visuddhi: Purity of conduct, purity of behaviour, purity of livelihood, purity of motive, purity of morals, purity of character.

Citta-visuddhi: Purity of mind, purity of all things mental, purity of mental attitude, purity of mental vision, purity of mental development, etc.

Diṭṭhi-visuddhi: Purity of faith, purity of thought, purity of intellect.

Kaṅkhāvitaraṇa-visuddhi: Purity of faith by the removal of doubt.

Maggāmaggañāṇadassana-visuddhi: Purity of the path by the true understanding of what is and what is not the path.

Paṭipadāñāṇadassana-visuddhi: Purity of the intellectual perception of the true path.

Ñāṇadassana-visuddhi: Purity of knowledge and insight.

The main items are really three: *Sīlavisuddhi* (Purity of morals), *Cittavisuddhi* (Purity of mind), and *Paññāvisuddhi* (Purity of knowledge).

The rough sketch of the Buddhist system of Purity was developed by Buddhadatta in his *Abhidhammāvatāra*, and more fully by Upatissa in his *Vimuttimagga*. The final development of the system took place in Buddhaghosa's *Visuddhimagga*. There is no other

Buddhist work which bears comparison with Buddhaghosa's Path of Purity in respect of thoroughness and painstaking analysis.

A General Buddhist View: — *Nirvāṇa* means the annihilation of passion, hatred, and delusion. It is the waning out of all evils — *rāga, dosa,* and *moha,* — the diminishing of the vicious and the weak in the man, which is the negative aspect of his positive advance in becoming (Mrs. Rhys Davids, *The Minor Anthologies*, I, p. xix). According to Childers, it means (1) the state of blissful sanctification of (wordly) existence in which Arhatship ends (*Dict. of the Pāli Language*, p. 266). In its negative aspect, it means the going out of greed, ill-will, and dullness, and also freedom from these; it may be variously described as 'comfort, end to ill, end of becoming, or life, end of craving and the rest'. In its positive aspect, and as subjectively considered, it means 'mental illumination conceived as light, insight, state of feeling happiness, and cool and calm and content (*sītibhāva, nibbuti, upasama*) peace, safety, and self-mastery'. Objectively considered, it means 'truth, the highest good, a supreme opportunity, a regulated life, communion with the Best, and bringing congenial work'. [1]

According to the *Khuddakapāṭha*, *Nirvāṇa* is immortality (*amata*) and the bliss of emancipation (*nibbuti*). It is the tranquil state (*santaṁ padaṁ*).

According to the *Dhammapada*, *Nirvāṇa* is immortality, the opposite of which is death. The path of action is the path to immortality, and the way of indolence is the way to death (*appamādo amatapadaṁ, pamādo maccuno padaṁ*). It is secure from the worldly contact, and unsurpassed in its reach. The path that leads to gain is one, and the path that leads to *Nirvāṇa*, another (*aññā hi lābhūpanisā, aññā nibbānagāminī*). The Buddhas declare the *Nirvāṇa* as the highest condition (*paramaṁ*). It is the greatest happiness (*paramaṁ sukhaṁ*). With the vision of *Nirvāṇa* the sinful nature vanishes for ever (*atthaṁ gacchanti āsavā*). Without knowledge there is no meditation, without meditation there is no knowledge; he who has knowledge and meditation is near unto *Nirvāṇa* (*yamhi jhānañ ca paññā ca, sa ve nibbāṇasantike*).

It is distinctly stated in the *Sutta-Nipāta*, that *Nirvāṇa* is a

[1] The characterization is based on The Psalms of the Early Buddhist Brethren and Sisters.

matchless island which possesses nothing, grasps at nothing, and which is the destroyer of decay and death (pp. 211—12) [1]. The world is bound by pleasure and by leaving desire *Nirvāṇa* can be attained (*Ibid.*, pp. 214—215).

According to the *Alīnacitta Jātaka* (II, Cowell, p. 17), one who possesses strong will, cherishes all good, takes to the Refuge and follows the path leading to *Nirvāṇa*, is capable of destroying all ties by slow degrees. The *Mora Jātaka* (Cowell, II, p. 26) describes *Nirvāṇa* as the only everlasting thing, and says that all other things being composite in their nature, are unsubstantial, transient, and subject to living and death. The *Gaṇḍatindu Jātaka* (Cowell, V, p. 55) says that zeal is the way to *Nirvāṇa*.

According to the *Visuddhimagga* (Vol. II, p. 612) *Nirvāṇa* is the extinction of the five *Khandhas* [2]. The attributes of *Nirvāṇa* consist of absence of passion, destruction of pride, getting rid of thirst, freedom from attachment and destruction of all sensual pleasures. It is the cessation of all sufferings. It can be attained through meditation, wisdom, precept, steadfastness, and the rest.

According to the *Atthasālinī* (p. 409), *Nirvāṇa* means that from which the arrow of desire is gone away (*taṇhā saṅkhātaṁ vāṇaṁ niggataṁ vā tasmā vāṇāti nibbānaṁ*). It is freedom from all sins and final release from lower nature.

In the *Sumaṅgalavilāsinī* (I, 217) Buddhaghosa says that a person obtains *Nirvāna* by making himself free from the wilderness of misdeeds. It is described here as the state of bliss.

In the *Kathāvatthupakaraṇa aṭṭhakathā* (p. 178) *Nirvāṇa* is described as a void [3].

According to the *Abhidhammatthasaṅgaha*, *Nirvāṇa* is so called because it is a departure from that craving which is called *vāṇa*, lusting or craving. It is to be realized through knowledge belonging to the four paths. It is the object of those paths and their fruition. It is supramundane or transcendental (*lokuttara*). It is excellent, uncreated, and free from lust.

According to Nāgasena's view in the *Milinda*, an *Ariyasāvaka*

---

[1] "*Ākiñcanaṃ anādānaṃ etaṃ dīpaṃ anāparaṃ nibbānaṃ iti naṃ brūmi jarāmaccuparikkhayaṃ*".

[2] *Pañcannaṃ Khandhānaṃ nirodho* (*Visuddhimagga, II, p.* 611).

[3] *Nibbānasaṁkhātāya Suññatāya.*

does not take pleasure in the senses and their objects. Inasmuch as he does not find delight in them, in him craving ceases, and by the cessation of craving (*taṇhā*) grasping (*upādāna*) ceases, and by the cessation of grasping, becoming (*bhava*) ceases, and when becoming has ceased, birth ceases, and with its cessation, birth, old age, and death, grief, lamentation, pain, sorrow, and despair cease to exist. In this sense cessation is *Nirvāṇa*.

Just as those whose hands and feet have not been cut off know how sad a thing it is to have them cut off, by hearing the sounds of the lamentation of those whose hands and feet have been cut off, even so, it is by hearing the pleasing words of those who have seen *Nirvāṇa* that they know how happy a state it is.

Nirvāṇa being uncaused, there is a cause that will bring about the realization of *Nirvāṇa*, but there is no cause that will bring about *Nirvāṇa* itself. A man by his ordinary power can go up from a certain place to the Himalayas, the king of mountains, but he cannot bring the Himalayas to his place. Such is the case with *Nirvāṇa*. Further, *Nirvāṇa* is uncompounded, not made of anything, yet it exists. It is perceptible to the mind. By means of his pure heart, refined and straight, free from the obstacles, free from low cravings, the disciple of the Noble One can realize *Nirvāṇa*. Just as wind exists, though it cannot be shown by its colour, or its form, whether as thin or thick, or short or long, even so *Nirvāṇa* exists, though it cannot be shown in colour or in form.

The supposed purity of infant mind is no comparison for the purity of consciousness in *Nirvāṇa*. The mind of one under seven years of age is powerless and weak, mean, small, slight, obscure and dull, whereas the condition of *Nirvāṇa* is transcendental, important, weighty, wide-reaching and extensive. The infant with imperfect mind is unable to grasp an idea so great.

Nirvāṇa is all bliss though the process seeking after it is painful. It is bliss unalloyed. When it is suggested that *Nirvāṇa* is painful, it is simply meant that the process of seeking after *Nirvāṇa* is painful, while *Nirvāṇa* itself is bliss, pure and simple, and there is no pain mixed with it.

Just as it is impossible to tell the measure of the water in the sea or the number of creatures dwelling therein, though, after all, the sea exists, so it is impossible to tell the form or figure or duration or measure of *Nirvāṇa*, though, after all, it is a condition that does exist. These are some of its characteristics. It is untarnished by evil dispositions. It is cool and assuages the fever arising from all evil dispositions. It does allay the thirst of the craving after lusts, the craving after future life, and the craving after wordly prosperity. It is the refuge of beings tormented with the poison of evil dispositions. It does put an end to grief. It is ambrosia. It is mighty and boundless, and fills not with all beings who enter into it. It is the abode of all 'good men' — the *Arahats*. It is all in blossom, as it were, with the innumerable and various and fine flowers of purity, of knowledge, and of emancipation. It is the support of life, for it puts an end to old age and death. It does increase the power of *iddhi* or supernormal powers. It puts a stop in all beings to the suffering arising from evil disposition. It overcomes in all beings the weakness which arises from hunger and every sort of pain. It is not born, neither does it grow old, it does not pass away, it has no rebirth, it is unconquerable, thieves cannot carry it, it is not attached to anything, it is the sphere in which *arahats* move, nothing can obstruct it, and it is infinite. It satisfies every desire. It causes delight. It is full of lustre. It is hard to attain to. It is unequalled in the beauty of its perfume. It is praised by all the Noble ones. It is beautiful in righteousness. It has the pleasant perfume of righteousness. It has a pleasant taste. It is very exalted. It is immoveable. It is inaccessible to sinners. It is a condition in which no evil dispositions can grow. It is free from desire to please and from resentment.

Nirvāṇa is neither past, nor future, nor present, nor produced, nor not-produced, nor producible.

Lastly, *Nirvāṇa* is to be known by freedom from distress and danger, by confidence, peace, calm, bliss, happiness, delicacy, purity and freshness. He who orders his life aright, realizes that *Nirvāṇa*. He who gains the highest fruit of Arahatship, may be said to have seen *Nirvāṇa*, face to face.

A layman also can attain *Nirvāṇa*. A close study of the *Guhaṭṭhaka-Sutta* (p. 58) and the *Jarā-Sutta* (p. 129) of the *Mahāniddesa* together with their commentaries by Dhammapāla helps up to look for the *munis* both among the householders and the recluses. The *munis* are defined as persons who have attenuated their sins and have seen *Nirvāṇa* and as to householders, they are represented as persons who are over-burdened with all household duties. No other discrimination is sought to be made between the *Āgāramunis* and the *Anāgāramunis* than this, that while the former keep to household life, the latter do not. As for the attainment, both are held out as equally competent to win the highest state, which is *Nirvāṇa* [1]. In the *Aṅguttara Nikāya*, we find mention of 21 lay *arahats* [2]. Rhys Davids in his introduction to the *Sāmaññaphala Sutta*, calls them laymen *arahats* (S.B.B., II, 63 fn.). In the *Kathāvatthu* (P.T.S., Bk. IV, p. 268), we find *Kulaputta* Yasa, householder Uttiya and young Brahman Setu attained arahatship in all the circumstances characterizing the life of the laity [3]. Referring to this point S. Z. Aung and Mrs. Rhys Davids have inferred that a layman under exceptional circumstances may attain arahatship but to keep it he must give up the world (*Points of Controversy*, p. 158 fn.). Rhys Davids and Mrs. Rhys Davids in Part III, p. 5 of the *Dialogues of the Buddha* (S.B.B., Vol. IV) have raised this question; who in the oldest period could be an *arahat*? The answer is: Any one — men or women, old or young, lay or *religieux*. It is distinctly mentioned in the *Milindapañha* that, whether he is a layman or a recluse, he who attains the supreme insight, to the supreme conduct of life, he too will win his way to the excellent condition of *arahatship*:

[1] *Āgāraṁ majjhe vasantā āgāramunino pabbajjūpagatā anāgāramunino sattasekkhamunino arahantā asekkhamunino paccekabuddhā paccekamunino sammāsambuddhā munimunino. Āgāramunino-Āgārikā ti kasigorakkhādi āgārikakamme niyuttā, diṭṭhapadāti diṭṭhanibbānā, viññātasāsanāti viññātaṁ sikkhattayasāsanaṁ etesanti viññātasāsanā. Anāgārā ti kasigorakkhādi āgāriyakammaṁ etesaṁ natthīti, pabbajjitā anāgārā ti vuccanti'* (*Commentary on the Mahāniddesa*, Siamese Edition, p. 218, *Guhaṭṭhaka Sutta and Jarā Sutta*).

[2] *Chahi bhikkhave dhammehi samannāgato Bhalliko gahapati .... Sudatto gahapati Anāthapiṇḍiko Citto gahapati Macchikāsaṇḍiko .... Hatthako Ālavako .... Mahānāmo Sakko .... Uggo gahapati Vesāliko .... Uggato gahapati .... Sūro Ambaṭṭho .... Jīvako Komārabhacco .... Nakulapitā gahapati .... Tavakaṇṇiko gahapati .... Purāṇo gahapati .... Isidatto gahapati .... Sandhāno gahapati .... Vijayo gahapati .... Vajjiyamahito gahapati .... Meṇḍako gahapati .... Vāseṭṭho upāsako, Ariṭṭho upāsako Sāraggo upāsako Tathāgate niṭṭhaṁ gato amataddaso amatam sacchikatvā, iriyati.* (*Aṅguttara Nikāya*, Vol. III, p. 451; Cf. *Vinaya*, I, 17).

[3] *Yaso kulaputto, Uttiyo gahapati, Setu māṇavo gihissa byañjanena arahattaṁ pattā, tena vata te vattabbe 'Gihī' ssa Arahā ti'.*

'Gihī pi mahārāja sammā-paṭipanno ārādhako hoti nāyaṁ dhammaṁ kusalaṁ, pabbajito pi mahārāja sammāpaṭipanno ārādhako hoti nāyaṁ dhammaṁ kusalaṁ'.

It is clear from this that the householder, if he leads a religious life, may attain to *arahatship* which is *nirvāṇa*. The *Milindapañha* further points out that whosoever has attained, as a layman, to *arahatship* one of the two courses is left to him and no other — either that very day he enters the Order, or he dies, for beyond that day he cannot last (*The Questions of King Milinda*, II, p. 96).

All persons who as laymen, living at home and in the enjoyment of the pleasures of senses, realize in themselves the condition of Peace, the Supreme Good *Nirvāṇa* — all of them had in former births accomplished their training, laid the foundation, in the practice of the thirteen vows, had purified their walk and conduct by means of them; and so now even as laymen, living at home and in the enjoyment of the pleasures of senses, they do realize in themselves the condition of Peace, the Supreme Good *Nirvāṇa* (*Ibid.*, II, p. 253).

INDEX